Workbook 5

Getting TQM to Work

Manage Activities
Diploma
S/NVQ Level 5

Institute of Management Open Learning Programme

Series editor: Gareth Lewis
Author: Annie Haight

im *the Institute*
of Management
F O U N D A T I O N

Pergamon
Open
Learning

Pergamon Open Learning
An imprint of Butterworth-Heinemann
Linacre House, Jordan Hill, Oxford OX2 8DP
A division of Reed Educational and Professional Publishing Ltd

ℛ A member of the Reed Elsevier plc group

OXFORD BOSTON JOHANNESBURG
MELBOURNE NEW DELHI SINGAPORE

First published 1997

British Library Cataloguing in Publication Data
A catalogue record for this book is available from the British Library

ISBN 0 7506 3664 5

Typeset by Avocet Typeset, Brill, Aylesbury, Bucks
Printed and bound in Great Britain

Contents

Series overview

The Institute of Management Open Learning Programme is a series of workbooks prepared by the Institute of Management and Pergamon Open Learning for managers seeking to develop themselves.

Comprising seventeen open learning workbooks, the programme covers the best of modern management theory and practice, and each workbook provides a range of frameworks and techniques to improve your effectiveness as a manager, thus helping you acquire the knowledge and skill to make you fully competent in your role.

Each workbook is written by an experienced management writer and covers an important management topic or theme. The activities both reinforce learning and help to relate the generic ideas to your individual work context. While coverage of each topic is fully comprehensive, additional reading suggestions and reference sources are given for those who wish to study to a greater depth.

Designed to be practical, stimulating and challenging, the aim of the workbooks is to improve performance at work by benefiting you and your organization. This practical focus is at the heart of the competence based approach that has been adopted by the programme.

The structure of the programme

The design and overall structure of the programme has two main organizing principles, both of which are closely linked to the national standards for management developed by the MCI (Management Charter Initiative).

First, the workbooks are grouped according to the key roles of management.

- Underpinning the management standards are a series of **personal competences** which describe the personal skills required by all managers, which are essential to skill in all the main functional or key role areas.
- **Manage Activities** describes the principles of managing processes and activities, with service to the customer as an essential part of this.
- **Manage Resources** describes the acquisition, control and monitoring of financial and other resources.
- **Manage People** looks at the key skills involved in leadership, developing one's staff and managing their performance.

■ **Manage Information** discusses the acquisition, storage and use of information for communication, problem solving and decision making.

In addition, there are three specialized key roles: **Manage Quality, Manage Projects** and **Manage Energy**. The workbooks cover the first two of these. Unlike the four primary key roles above, these are not compulsory for certificate, diploma or S/NVQ requirements, but provide options for the latter.

Together, these key roles provide a comprehensive description of the fundamental principles of management as it applies in any organization – commercial, maintained sector or not-for-profit.

Second, the programme is organized according to **levels of management**, seniority and responsibility.

Level 4 represents first line management. In accredited programmes this is equivalent to S/NVQ Level 4, Certificate in Management or CMS. Level 5 is equivalent to middle/senior management and is accredited at S/NVQ Level 5, Diploma in Management or DMS. There are two S/NVQs at Level 5: Operational Management and Strategic Management. The operations role is focussed internally within an organization on the maintenance of systems and standards of output, whilst the strategic role is focussed on the whole organization, including the external operating environment, and looks at setting directions.

Together, the workbooks cover all the background knowledge you need to have for all units of competence in the MCI standards at Level 4 and Level 5 (apart from the specialized units in the key role Manage Energy). They also provide skills development and opportunities for portfolio building.

For a comprehensive list of workbooks, see page ix. For a comprehensive list of links with the standards, see the *User Guide*.

How to use the programme

The programme is deliberately designed to be flexible and can be used in a variety of ways:

■ to update on important management topics and themes, or develop individual skills: as the workbooks are grouped according to themes, it should be easy for you to pick out one that suits your needs

■ as part of generic management development programmes: you can choose the modules that fit the themes of the programme

■ as part of, and in support of, accredited competence-based programmes.

For N/SVQs at both Levels 4 and 5, there are options in the combinations of units that make up the various awards. By using the map provided in the *User Guide*, individuals will be able to select the workbooks appropriate to their specific needs, and their chosen accreditation options. Some of the activities will help you provide evidence for your portfolio; where we think this is the case, we give the relevant reference to the standards.

For Certificate or CMS, Diploma or DMS, individuals should choose modules that not only meet their individual needs but also satisfy the requirements of the delivering body and the awarding body.

You may need help and guidance in these choices, and the *User Guide* sets out the options and advice in much more detail. A fuller description of the potential uses of this material in evidence gathering and portfolio building can also be found in the *User Guide*, as can a detailed description of the contents of each workbook.

Workbooks in the Institute of Management Open Learning Programme

Personal Competences (Levels 4 and 5)

   1 *The Influential Manager**
   2 *Managing Yourself**

Manage Activities (Level 4)

   3 *Understanding Business Process Management*
   4 *Customer Focus*

Manage Activities (Level 5)

   5 *Getting TQM to Work*
   6 *Leading from the Front*
   7 *Improving Your Organization's Success*

Manage Resources (Level 4)

   8 *Project Management*
   9 *Budgeting and Financial Control*

Manage Resources (Level 5)

   10 *Effective Financial and Resource Management*

Manage People (Level 4)

   1 *The Influential Manager*
   2 *Managing Yourself*
   11 *Getting the Right People to do the Right Job*
   12 *Developing Yourself and Your Staff*
   13 *Building a High Performance Team*

An asterisk indicates that a particular workbook also contains material suitable for a particular key role or personal competence over and above that where it is principally designated.

Links to qualifications

S/NVQ programmes

This workbook can help candidates to achieve credit and develop skills in the key role of Manage Activities at Level 5, and covers the following units and elements:

A3   Manage activities to meet customer requirements
A3.1   Agree customer requirements
A3.2   Plan activities to meet customer requirements
A3.3   Provide a healthy, safe and productive work environment
A3.4   Ensure products and services meet customer requirements
A5   Manage change in organizational activities
A5.1   Identify opportunities for improvements in activities
A5.2   Evaluate proposed changes for benefits and disadvantages
A5.3   Plan the implementation of change in activities
A5.4   Agree the introduction of change
A5.5   Implement changes in activities
F4   Implement quality assurance systems
A6.1   Establish quality assurance systems
A6.2   Maintain quality assurance systems
A6.3   Recommend improvements to quality assurance systems

It can also help candidates to achieve credit and develop skills in the key role of Manage Quality at Level 5, and covers the following units and elements:

Fl   Promote the importance and benefits of quality
F1.1   Promote the importance of quality in the organization's strategy
Fl.2   Promote quality throughout the organization and its customer and supplier networks
F3   Manage continuous quality improvement
F3.1   Develop and implement systems to monitor and evaluate organizational performance
F3.2   Promote continuous quality improvement for products, services and processes
F4   Implement quality assurance systems
F4.1   Establish quality assurance systems
F4.2   Maintain quality assurance systems
F4.3   Recommend improvement to quality assurance systems
F6   Monitor compliance with quality systems
F6.1   Plan to audit compliance with quality systems
F6.2   Implement the audit plan
F6.3   Report on compliance with quality systems

Certificate and Diploma programmes

This workbook, together with the other level 5 workbooks on managing activities (6 – *Leading from the Front* and 7 – *Improving your Organization's Success*), covers all of the knowledge required in the key role Manage Activities for Diploma and DMS programmes. It also covers all of the knowledge required for units in the key role Manage quality.

Links to other workbooks

Other workbooks in the key role Manage Activities at level 5 are:

6 *Leading from the Front*

7 *Improving your Organization's Success*

and at Level 4:

3 *Understanding Business Process Management*
4 *Customer Focus*

Introduction

What's in it for you?

TQM – Total Quality Management – has been a management buzz word in the UK for over a decade. Before that, it was made famous by vanguard organizations in the United States such as Hewlett Packard, IBM, Xerox and Motorola, who used it to beat back the vigorous business challenge mounted by Japanese corporations in the late 1970s and early 1980s.

Total Quality Management is a business approach that emphasizes an all-out commitment to quality, most memorably defined as 'delighting the customer'. It is well known for its use of technical methods such as measurement and process management, and of certain Japanese-inspired ways of people management, such as quality circles.

One of the characteristics of TQM is its emphasis on an absolute value: the organization's need for total commitment to the highest possible standards, which has often been expressed in slogans such as 'zero defects' and 'do it right first time, every time'. This absolutism has sometimes been translated by advocates into extravagant claims that Total Quality Management is the formula for Total Success.

In fact there have been a number of significant success stories for TQM in the UK, including Rank Xerox, ICL, Short Brothers and Jaguar. There have also been a number of quiet – and some not-so-quiet – failures. In the latter half of 1996, for example, postal workers viewed the Royal Mail's TQM initiative as the company's excuse for encroaching further on already-eroded working conditions. The result was a series of strikes which injured customers and the organization.

TQM has been around for some time and its track record has been chequered. Isn't it old hat? Hasn't its claim to be the universal management panacea been disproved, not only by its failures, but also by the emergence of newer ideas such as Business Process Re-engineering? In the run-up to the millennium, why should managers consider initiating TQM programmes in their organizations?

The answer is one that most managers know quite well already: Management by Flavour of the Month is never a good idea. If the Holy Grail of management existed, it would have been found by now. The plain truth is: there is no universal panacea. Whatever claims TQM has made to being one must be discounted along with all the other promises of miracle cures.

To dismiss TQM as just another fashion, however, is both inaccurate and unfair. Total Quality Management is based on solid, balanced management principles. It has produced significant, demonstrable results in a number of cases. Where it has failed, its failures may be analysed for common errors of implementation such as:

- insufficient support from top management
- unrealistic timescales
- lack of commitment to the necessary cultural changes in the organization
- inadequate people management skills
- lack of follow-through in process management

The acid test for considering a TQM initiative is whether or not your organization can benefit from one, and this is determined by how far down the path to quality your organization has travelled. While a number of progressive, pioneering companies in turbulent markets took up TQM in the first wave of implementation, not all companies did so. There is still plenty of scope for many organizations in both the private sector and the public services, in both manufacturing and service industries, to profit from the benefits of TQM. These include:

- its unwavering focus on customers
- its view of the organization as a total system whose activities can be optimized
- its rigorous analysis and improvement of processes
- its practical, empowering approaches to managing people

Organizations introducing TQM at present are in a better position now than the pioneering companies in earlier years, because they can learn from other organizations' successes and failures.

One important test of the validity of Total Quality Management is that the management methods which have followed in its wake are based on TQM principles. Newer approaches such as Business Process Improvement, Redesign, or Re-engineering are based on the measurement, process control and corrective action techniques advanced by TQM, as well as on its philosophy of continuous improvement. These methods don't replace Total Quality Management, but rather extend it.

This workbook can help you decide whether TQM is right for your organization. It is designed to lead you through the key ideas and major issues, and to help you anticipate and prepare for the implications of implementing Total Quality Management in your organization. You will find examples illustrating how other companies have handled the TQM challenge. Finally, the structured activities will help you build up your own expertise and your own way of approaching TQM in your organization.

Objectives

By the end of this workbook you should be able to:

■ understand the concept of quality, the principles of TQM, and the major approaches

■ identify factors that promote or inhibit TQM initiatives

■ plan for the introduction of TQM

■ understand the importance of culture, communication and commitment

■ use various approaches to influencing staff and colleagues

■ use technical skills to implement and evaluate quality initiatives

■ use processes to monitor quality and evaluate results

Section 1 TQM: The basics

Introduction

This section of the workbook gives you an overview of Total Quality Management. It outlines the main principles and philosophy of TQM, and relates these to the two main strands of the TQM approach: technical process management and human resource management. It overviews the general process an organization follows when introducing a Total Quality Management programme. Finally, it identifies some of the critical factors which promote or inhibit the successful introduction of TQM initiatives.

What is quality?

Any consideration of Total Quality Management must start with a definition of quality. But formulating a definition that works for every organization can be tricky. What do a small hairdressing salon, a major university, a cinema and an electricity-generating plant have in common? They all have **customers**.

One of the most important developments in the evolution of quality thinking from its beginnings in the 1920s to the present, is that quality is primarily defined not in terms of adherence to a specification, but in terms of what the customer wants (Figure 1). As the CEO of one Total Quality organization put it, 'Quality is what our customers say it is.' This healthy shift of focus has allowed the application of quality concepts to a much wider range of organizations (including service organizations and public sector organizations) and a much wider range of activities (including administrative and managerial activities). In public service organizations, the concept of stakeholders is often substituted for the idea of customers, but, in general, the effect is the same.

H. J. Harrington, a leading American quality analyst, suggests that quality should be defined as:

Meeting or exceeding customer expectations, at a price that represents value for money to them, and delivering your product or service when they need it.[1]

Relies on inspection to deliver consistent product	Relies on operations management to ensure consistent product	Relies on satisfying customer requirements through holistic process management
Quality control	Quality assurance	Total Quality Management
1920s	1950s	1970s	1990s

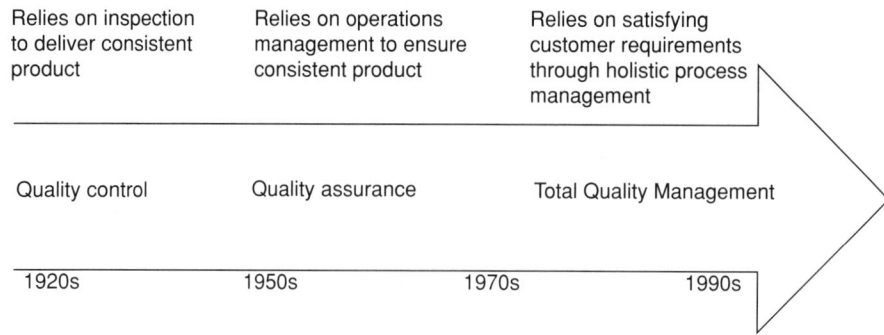

Figure 1   The evolution of quality concepts

Customers' expectations include not only the features of the products or services they buy, but all-important aspects of customer service such as courtesy and product knowledge as well. These intangible elements are encompassed in the pithiest definition of quality:

Quality is delighting the customer.

ACTIVITY 1   A3

    1   Does your organization have a general, organization-wide definition of quality? If so, write it down here.

    2   Fill out the following form as far as you can. You can address your customers' general expectations, or relate the exercise to a particular product or service.

Customer-focus analysis form

Our customers' expectations are:

We know this because:

This information was collected in the following way:

This information was collected _____ months ago. It will be updated in _____ months.

We are taking the following action on this information:

FEEDBACK

Did you know this information? If not, you will have an opportunity to address these issues further in Section 2, which focuses on an assessment of where your organization is on the path to quality.

WHAT DOES QUALITY MEAN TO AN ORGANIZATION?

There are a number of advantages to pursuing quality as a business strategy. In the present complex and rapidly changing environment, customers tend to be sophisticated and demanding. As Allen Paison, President of Walker

Customer Satisfaction Measurement commented, 'Customers today want quality and value in the products and services they buy. Moreover, they usually can find it, and tend to look until they do.'[2] Organizations that fail to deliver quality are on the road to extinction.

Organizations that compete on quality rather than price can avoid the business suicide caused by destructive price wars. Running high-quality systems internally ensures cost-effective operations which maximize profits and allow efficiency savings to be passed along to customers. In the United Kingdom and the rest of Europe, Total Quality initiatives have been used to streamline operations, increase productivity, cut costs and expand market share. Quality means:

- survival
- competitiveness
- success

ACTIVITY 2

What could a Total Quality programme do for your organization? Jot down a few ideas on the main advantages you see for pursuing Total Quality.

FEEDBACK

Of course, answers are likely to be individual, but advantages of quality programmes are discussed below, and should be read as a basis for comparison.

BS 5750 and ISO 9000

BS 5750 and ISO 9000 are the quality assurance standards of the British Standards Institute and the International Standards Organization, who have developed a detailed programme and guidance through which organizations can seek accreditation to these standards. A detailed discussion of these standards is outside the remit of this workbook, but you should be aware of their relationship to Total Quality Management.

Essentially, the process of seeking and gaining accreditation to these standards demonstrates a serious commitment to quality assurance and is a good indication that an organization has progressed some way down the path to quality. On the other hand, BS 5750/ISO 9000 does not transform an organization into a Total Quality organization. This can only be done through a carefully managed programme specifically tailored for the individual organization, which integrates the principles of TQM in a holistic way with the full range of its activities.

It is also worth noting that an organization can be a successful Total Quality organization without accreditation to the BSI/ISO standards. In short, the standards and the route to Total Quality Management are separate, but parallel, processes.

The principles of Total Quality Management

This section looks briefly at the main principles of TQM. A number of management experts have contributed to the concepts and philosophy of Total Quality Management, and the ideas of the most important gurus are outlined in the Appendix. For now, we will examine the most important principles of TQM in overview.

PUT THE CUSTOMER FIRST

This is the golden rule of the Total Quality approach. It involves thinking like a customer: finding out what customers want, putting their needs and desires first, and thinking backwards through the organization's systems to ensure excellence of delivery.

Customers can be internal or external

A customer can be defined as the recipient of an output or activity. Of course this includes external customers who purchase a product or service. It also includes internal customers, the people inside the organization who are the next link in the process chain. This means that everyone in the organization is linked in supplier–customer relationships, with all the responsibilities for customer satisfaction that this entails.

Examples of internal customers include people who use the reprographics department, or warehouse packers who receive customer orders from the sales department. The reprographics customers need copies to be legible, with the pages in the right order, and securely stapled. The warehouse packers – the customers of the sales department – need order forms to be legible and accurate, and to include complete information such as the customer's post code. If these quality requirements are not met, it causes the internal customer problems, frustration, and time and increases the organization's costs.

ACTIVITY 3

Who are the customers for your outputs at work? Try to identify three types of internal customers, for the various types of outputs you are responsible for in your organization.

1

2

3

Looking at organizational activities in terms of internal customers can be surprisingly revolutionary in that it tends to subvert the familiar patterns of both organizational hierarchy and functional divisions. In other words it cuts across organizational structure both vertically and horizontally (Figure 2).

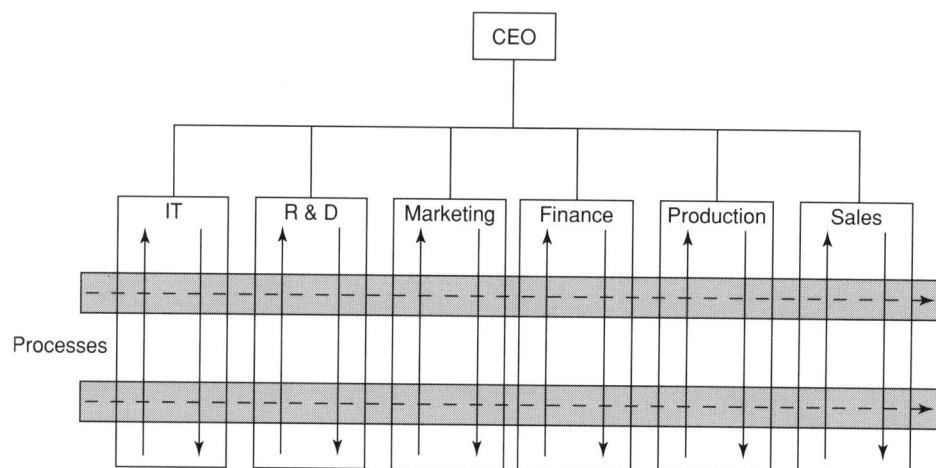

Figure 2 Relationships between internal suppliers and customers can cut across both vertical and horizontal boundaries

For example, one internal customer of a high-ranking senior manager may be his or her secretary, who has legitimate cause for complaint if she is expected to work from indecipherable handwriting. This would be an example of the supplier–customer relationship cutting across vertical levels of an organization's hierarchy.

Customer–supplier relationships can also cross functional (horizontal) boundaries. An example of this would be when the finance department receives financial information from a number of different budget-holding centres during its annual budget preparation. In this case, the finance department is the customer and the budget centres are the suppliers.

Organizations are customers too

An important element of the customer-first approach is the organization's need to become a more demanding customer itself. External suppliers are vitally important to the smoothness and quality of an organization's processes. An organization pursuing Total Quality can not afford bought-in supplies, components, or services being substandard. Such organizations often renegotiate their relationship with external suppliers, working with and accrediting a small number of excellent, reliable suppliers. With such suppliers, customer organizations tend to develop close, co-operative relationships, which often includes elements such as:

- advice and assistance in specifying standards and designing processes
- joint training initiatives
- just-in-time delivery

ACTIVITIES AS PROCESSES

Systems theory, developed in the 1960s, allows any activity to be analysed as a process, which takes in inputs, acts on them, and delivers outputs. This model (Figure 3) can apply to any process, from the simplest, such as ringing up a purchase on a till, to the most complex, such as launching a rocket into space. (Complex processes are made up of a number of interlocking sub-processes.)

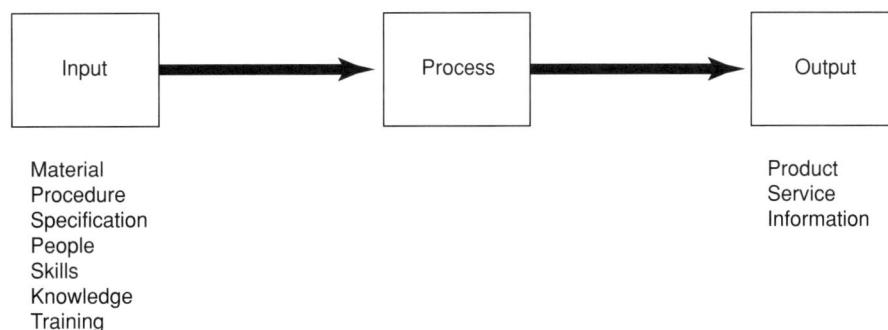

```
┌─────────┐         ┌─────────┐         ┌─────────┐
│  Input  │ ──────▶ │ Process │ ──────▶ │ Output  │
└─────────┘         └─────────┘         └─────────┘

Material                                  Product
Procedure                                 Service
Specification                             Information
People
Skills
Knowledge
Training
```

Figure 3   The process model

The advantage of viewing organizational activities as processes is that processes can be analysed, measured, managed, and improved. One fundamental strand of Total Quality Management is the use of highly developed process management techniques for achieving this. Workbook 3 in this series, *Understanding Business Process Management*, is an excellent introduction to this subject, which is also discussed further in Section 5 of this workbook.

'QUALITY IS FREE'

This maxim, from quality guru Philip Crosby, can seem both contentious and confusing. Certainly quality is not free if you don't already have it. For example, introducing and running a Total Quality initiative is not free. Cost effective, yes. Providing excellent value for money and return on investment, yes. Free, no.

Crosby's point is easier to understand if we turn his statement on its head, and say that lack of quality is expensive. Compared to the costs of poor quality – which include loss of market share and higher operating costs – maintaining quality systems is free. Once they are up and running, systems and operations producing defect-free, high-quality output, are, in effect, providing quality for free.

PREVENTION IS BETTER THAN CURE ...

... and much, much cheaper. Quality costs, or more accurately, poor-quality costs, fall into three general areas:

- prevention costs, which include resources spent on ensuring that deviations from quality don't occur
- appraisal costs, which include the costs of inspecting both suppliers' materials and the organization's own output to ensure conformity to specification
- failure costs, including the costs of scrap, reworking, handling customer complaints, warranties, servicing, replacements and refunds

Of these costs, prevention costs are by far the lowest. For example, it costs five times less to retain a satisfied customer (that is, to prevent a customer defection) than to find a new customer. The further a mistake travels toward the final, external customer, the greater its costs escalate. (See Figure 4.)

The cost to organizations of having poor quality has been estimated at between 15 and 40 per cent of turnover. These costs can be slashed by introducing Total Quality Management. According to Harrington, 'It is reasonable to expect poor-quality cost to be cut 30 percent over a 3-year period after the improvement process is fully implemented.'[3]

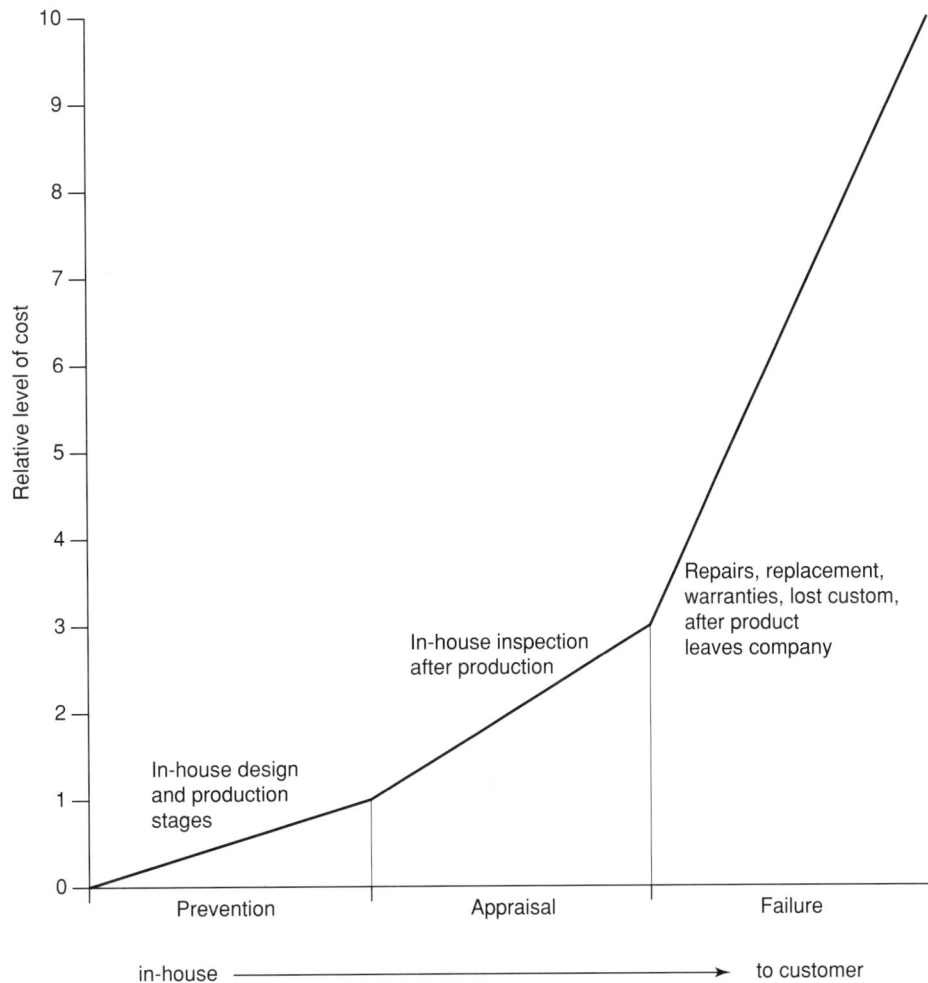

Figure 4   Relative values of prevention, appraisal, and failure costs

---

ACTIVITY 4

Do you know how much poor quality costs your organization each year?

REDUCE VARIATION AND AIM FOR ZERO DEFECTS

Deviation from quality is the result of variation from a required standard or specification. In a technical sense, improving quality is a matter of reducing variation. Systems should be designed – and employees trained and empowered – to deliver a performance level of 'zero defects' (another of Crosby's terms). While attaining absolute perfection is unlikely, it is important to aim for it, as this is most likely to enable the organization to achieve the highest quality possible.

QUALITY IS EVERYONE'S RESPONSIBILITY

For Total Quality to work, it must be embedded at the heart of the organization. This means making employees at all levels accountable for the quality of their work. It also means creating working conditions which give them the power to achieve quality, for example, giving assembly line workers the authority to reject a substandard part or to stop production lines if variations reach a certain critical level. Quality initiatives should enable the organization to tap the creativity and experience of every employee.

The Total Quality approach poses particular challenges to managers, because it requires them to consult and listen to employees, act on the problems they identify, and devolve authority to them. Total Quality often demands a cultural change in the organization, in which managers must redefine their roles and use a more participative, empowering management style. Total Quality initiatives will be unsuccessful unless one of their goals is to produce a significant improvement in the quality of employees' working lives.

ACTIVITY 5   A3, FI

How many of the principles of TQM are consciously promoted and followed in your organization at the moment?

In the following table, identify evidence which demonstrates the importance of each principle to your organization. Evaluate the evidence for the level of commitment to the principle that it illustrates. In the Rating column:

- write 0 if there is no evidence relating the principle to the organization
- write 1 if the evidence demonstrates an awareness of the principle
- write 2 if the evidence demonstrates unofficial, piecemeal efforts to implement the principle
- write 3 if the evidence demonstrates systematic, organization-wide procedures and processes designed to put the principle into practice

Principle	Evidence of importance in my organization	Rating
Putting the customer first		
Seeing activities as processes		
Reducing poor-quality costs		
Reducing variation		
Preventing, not rectifying, mistakes		
Making quality everyone's responsibility		

Running a TQM programme: An overview

As with any change management programme, planning and running a TQM initiative follows a general sequence of steps:

- pre-planning
- planning
- communicating and gaining commitment
- implementation
- review

The steps illustrated in Figure 5 are outlined below.

PRE-PLANNING

This is the phase in which senior managers begin to consider whether a quality improvement programme could benefit their organization. Some organizations enter this phase proactively, as part of normal strategic planning. Others come to it reactively, in response to a business crisis such as the critical need to reduce costs, increase productivity, or respond to a new competitive threat.

Usually, a small team of middle and senior managers is given the task of investigating the issue of quality improvement and assessing its strategic potential for the organization. Activities at this stage include:

- recognizing the need for a quality initiative
- assessing the costs and benefits to the organization
- deciding whether or not to commit resources to initiate a TQM programme

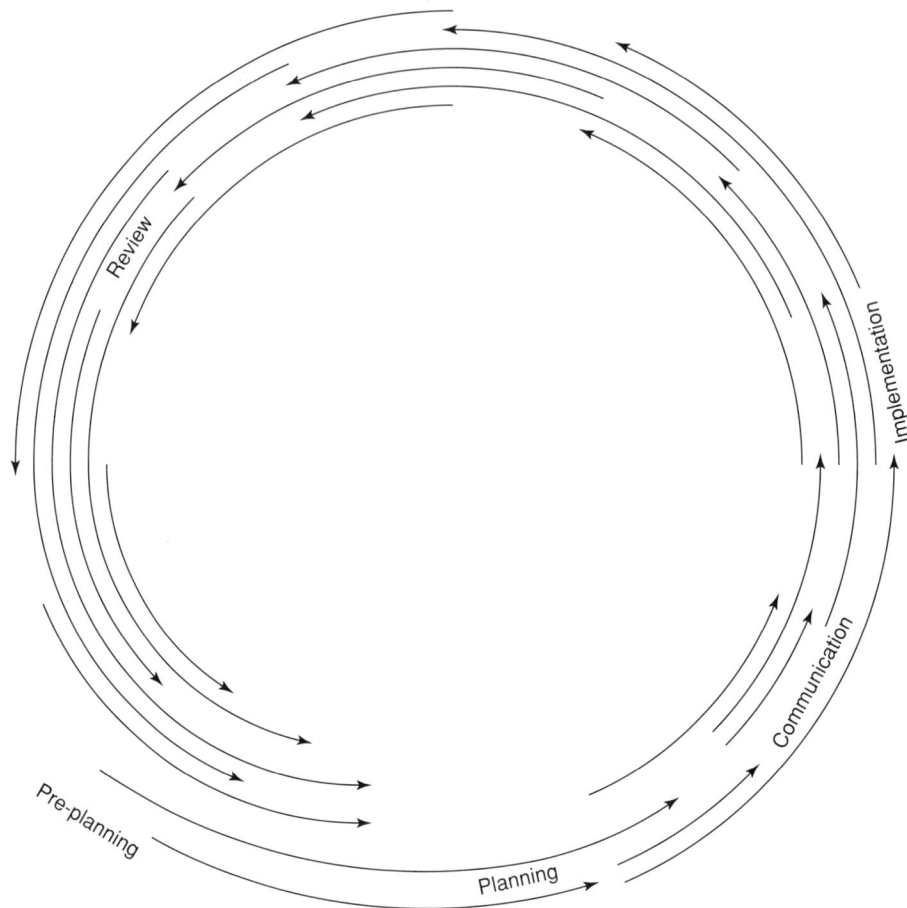

Figure 5   Overview of the TQM process

PLANNING

This is the stage at which the organization has decided to plan seriously to introduce a TQM programme. A carefully selected project team, with representatives from each functional area, work with an internal change agent, and, usually, with an external management consultancy. Activities at this stage include:

- gathering and analysing information from customers, suppliers and relevant members of the organization
- deciding priorities
- choosing a quality guru whose method the organization will adopt
- benchmarking against other organizations
- setting targets and milestones
- developing detailed plans and schedules to achieve them

COMMUNICATING AND GAINING COMMITMENT

At some point during the planning phase the organization needs to begin an initial publicity campaign for the TQM initiative. A publicity campaign should usually overlap with the planning phase, so that input from members of the organization can be considered by the planning team and fed into the planning process. Communication means two-way dialogue, listening as well as telling.

A publicity campaign initially involves informing all members of the organization about the intention to introduce a quality programme. It continues through out the implementation stage, updating employees on developments and successes. A variety of media, ranging from the company newsletter to posters to personal letters from the managing director, can be used. The campaign must be designed to gain commitment to the TQM programme from every level of the organization. It runs concurrently with training programmes which should cascade from top management, through middle management and supervisory layers, to shop-floor level. Activities in this phase involve:

- consulting with employees at all levels
- analysing organizational culture and developing strategies to change it, if necessary
- campaigning to win 'hearts and minds' to the TQM programme as a meaningful way forward for the organization
- suggestion schemes to generate ideas for improving quality

IMPLEMENTATION

Implementation of a Total Quality Management programme involves two vital and interdependent aspects:

- human resource elements
- technical elements

Human resource elements

These focus on creating the interpersonal skills and corporate climate necessary to sustain the initiative. Activities in this area include:

- training in participative management skills for all managerial and supervisory levels
- training of front-line employees in communication skills and in running effective quality team meetings

- facilitation of quality team meetings by line managers and HR staff
- finding and introducing ways of using the quality programme to boost morale

Technical elements

These are the 'hard' skills and activities needed to effect process changes which result in the elimination of variation and defects, and a significant increase in quality. Activities in this area include:

- training in problem-solving techniques and the technical skills of process management for all managers, supervisors and relevant employees
- measuring and analysing processes
- quality team meetings
- problem-solving and process improvement (which may include process redesign or re-engineering)

Review

Continuous improvement is one of the defining characteristics of the Total Quality approach, so any TQM programme needs to be regularly reviewed to assess its effectiveness, maintain momentum, and identify further opportunities for making improvements.

The review procedure should also provide an opportunity for the organization to share and celebrate successes and to investigate ways of reusing successful ideas in other parts of the organization. Recycling intellectual capital is an important means of recouping initial expenditure on the quality initiative. Finding creative ways of reusing good ideas is an important source of quality gains in organizations with successful TQM programmes.

Activities in the phase include:

- assessing new process measures to determine effectiveness
- identifying and measuring quality gains
- analysing both successes and failures for the lessons they teach
- recommending adjustments or improvements to new measures
- identifying further applications for successful ideas
- identifying further areas needing improvement

ACTIVITY 6

What stage would you say your organization has reached in the process of running a TQM programme?

TQM: How it succeeds, why it fails

THE RISKS AND REWARDS

Total Quality Management is not a low-risk strategy. Managers of organizations considering adopting the TQM approach need to carefully weigh up the possible risks and rewards, to decide whether it is right for them.

The advantages of a successful TQM initiative include:

- satisfied or delighted customers
- high morale among employees at all levels: job satisfaction, pride and enjoyment
- improved relationships with suppliers
- increased productivity
- reductions in poor-quality costs
- retaining or extending market share
- the ability to attract and retain high-quality employees
- the optimization of resources including the creativity and loyalty of employees

The disadvantages of Total Quality Management can include:

- cost: instituting a quality initiative requires investment, which may not begin to show returns for two to three years
- time: instituting a successful quality initiative requires up to two years
- short- to medium-term decreases in productivity; during implementation, employees at all levels will spend significant time away from their ordinary jobs in order to focus on their part of the quality initiative
- its requirement for emotional energy, commitment, faith and trust
- its potential to create bureaucracy and increase paperwork
- the 'burnt bridges' factor: with TQM there is no going back to old habits or procedures
- the risk that a failed initiative can seriously damage morale

CONDITIONS THAT FOSTER SUCCESS

In the 1980s, Tom Peters estimated that up to 98 per cent of quality initiatives fail. Fortunately, experience of TQM programmes during the last decade in the United Kingdom (and even longer in the United States) has led experts and practitioners to a number of conclusions about why such initiatives succeed or fail. Nowadays, managers launching a quality initiative have a greater chance of success if they are willing to learn from other organizations' mistakes and triumphs.

Three important factors which make for success have been identified:

- organizational culture
- leadership and management style
- organizational ability to consolidate and apply new learning

Organizational culture is a critical issue for successful TQM programmes. Organizations which already have a favourable culture will find that the implementation of TQM progresses more smoothly. Organizations that do not have a favourable culture will have a rougher ride, but can still be successful if they act on the understanding that fundamentally changing the culture is an essential, perhaps *the* essential, prerequisite for success.

A favourable organizational culture is one in which there is a reasonable degree of trust and communication:

- among managers and
- between management and the workforce

Morale is high. Departmental fortresses have not been allowed to grow up and create suspicion, jealousy or hostility between functional divisions. Generally such organizations have a progressive, best-practice attitude to human resource management and development.

In short, the organization has already absorbed and put into practice a number of the 'soft' skills on which TQM draws so heavily. Good foundations are already in place for further advances in the areas of shop-floor consultation, teamwork, and two-way communication both horizontally, between departments, and vertically, between the hierarchical levels of the organization.

One vital influence on culture is leadership and management style. Successful TQM initiatives tend to have 'forthright but listening' leaders.[4] Their management style tends to be participative rather than autocratic or authoritarian. The most fortunate organizations have the benefit of transformational leaders, who can inspire or provoke change rather than impose it. Such leaders make it clear that, while attaining quality is a non-negotiable goal, the journey to quality is a collective adventure for the organization. They generate excitement about the change programme, and involve all levels of the organization in defining and pursuing quality. In this way, quality is integrated into the heart of the organization, rather than remaining a faddish add-on.

The final success factor relates to the ability of the organization to become a 'learning organization'. There are two aspects to this issue:

- creating a learning environment
- consolidating gains

Establishing a learning environment involves creating a climate where employees are allowed to learn by doing, where theoretical training is always tied in to working practice. Research confirms that people learn best when they feel safe. Employees must be allowed time for learning by experimentation, in a safe atmosphere where risk taking is encouraged and failure is accepted without blame or ridicule. This is the best environment for encouraging creativity and innovation and the one most likely to produce substantive quality improvements.

Innovation and learning are unlikely to result in bottom-line gains, however, unless the organization has a relentless commitment to apply and integrate them into every part of the organization that could benefit. For example, it is no good for the IT department to develop a powerful database system which the marketing and sales departments cannot be persuaded to use. Quality improvements must be driven by the commitment to find practical, workable applications and implement them as widely as possible across the organization.

CONDITIONS THAT LEAD TO FAILURE

As you might expect, the absence of any of the success factors outlined previously will tend to hamper the success of a TQM initiative. Initiatives often founder because top management does not have the will, or commit the resources, fundamentally to change the existing organizational culture, if it works against the Total Quality philosophy.

Often, 'soft', people management skills are not sufficiently well developed for an organization to cope successfully with the transition to TQM. Inappropriate attitudes and practices of management at all levels can seriously impede success. It is well known that senior management must be absolutely committed to change initiatives, and this is certainly true in the case of Total Quality programmes. Less emphasized, but equally important, is the attitude of front-line management and supervisory staff. Certain elements of the TQM approach may be threatening to this section of the organization. If they are not convinced of what's in it for them, and trained in the necessary skills, they can scupper a quality initiative. Finally, employees may see TQM (sometimes correctly) as a path to redundancies, and so fail to co-operate. One expert, H. J. Harrington, believes that there has to be a 'no redundancies' policy for TQM initiatives to work.[5]

One American study concluded that, in many organizations, the transfer from quality theory to practice never occurred effectively because quality gurus, management consultants and the organization's management itself over-estimated the workforce's existing abilities in communication and problem-solving skills. Initiatives that set the starting point of training programmes at too sophisticated a level are courting failure.[6]

Selecting the wrong TQM model can also be a hazard. Total Quality Management is a general, 'umbrella' term for a number of approaches (all focused on achieving quality) developed by different management gurus. Certain models are more appropriate for certain types of organization. (For example, Crosby's approach tends to be more appropriate for manufacturing companies.) Organizations (usually assisted by a management consultant) must select their TQM approach carefully, ensuring that it matches their organization's goals and activities, and stick to it. Changing horses in mid-stream is not a good idea.

Problems can also be caused when there is an imbalance between the 'hard', technical and 'soft', people skills necessary to implement TQM. For a quality initiative to work, neither set of skills must be emphasized at the expense of the other, and both must be developed to work in tandem.

Finally, the experts warn that quality programmes can fail because timescales are unrealistic and consequently insufficient resources are devoted to the process of introducing them.

ACTIVITY 6

On the force-field analysis form below, take an initial stab at identifying the factors hindering and promoting TQM in your organization. This is a preliminary exercise designed to get you thinking about these issues, which will be explored at greater length in later parts of the workbook.

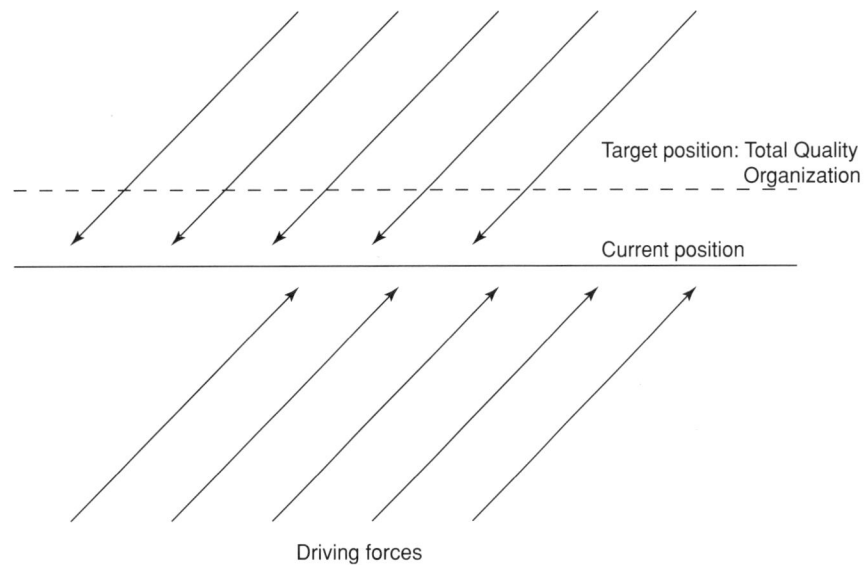

Target position: Total Quality Organization

Current position

Driving forces

FEEDBACK

How you might tackle these issues – particularly the inhibiting forces, is dealt with in Sections 3 and 4.

The following activity helps you to consolidate your learning in this section.

ACTIVITY 7

1 Give a working definition of quality which could be applied to virtually any organization.

2 Explain the term 'process chain'.

3 What are the implications of putting the customer first? List three or four.

4 What is an internal customer?

5 Why is prevention better than cure, in quality terms?

6 Explain the terms 'reducing variation' and 'zero defects'.

7 What are the five general stages involved in running a TQM programme?

8 List five advantages and five disadvantages of pursuing a TQM approach.

9 What are the two major elements involved in running a successful TQM programme?

10 List three factors which promote success in introducing a TQM initiative.

11 List four common reasons why quality initiatives tend to fail.

FEEDBACK

If you had difficulties with any question in the previous activity, refresh your memory by re-reading the relevant section. Or you might find it useful to discuss the issue with a colleague.

Summary

- Total Quality Management is a holistic management approach concerned with promoting quality as the cornerstone of an organization's activities. The focus of the TQM approach is pleasing the customer. Thus, quality may be defined as satisfying or surpassing customer expectations. Pursuing quality as a business strategy has a number of potential advantages, including expanding market share, cutting costs and increasing customer and employee satisfaction.
- Total Quality Management depends on putting into practice several important principles. Pleasing customers – whether external or internal – becomes the primary focus of the organization's efforts. In keeping with the holistic nature of TQM, quality must become the responsibility of everyone in the organization.
- Activities are managed as processes, having inputs, actions and outputs; this allows them to be measured, analysed and improved. The lack of quality, in terms of defects, errors and inefficiencies, is costly to an organization. The most efficient way of paring poor-quality costs is to prevent, rather than rectify, defects (understood as variations from quality standards).
- Managing Total Quality depends on the effective use of two separate but interdependent sets of skills. 'Hard' or technical skills, are employed to analyse processes, solve problems, and generate and evaluate improvements. 'Soft' or people management skills are used to gain commitment and input from employees at every level of the organization. Without the competent use of both types of skills, TQM initiatives can fail.

■ Introducing a TQM programme can take up to two years and follows the general pattern of instituting any change programme. It includes phases of pre-planning, planning, communicating and gaining commitment, implementation, and review. Often several of these phases run concurrently.

■ A TQM initiative tends to be most successful if the organization either already has, or makes a top priority of creating, a culture in which trust, healthy morale and participative, democratic styles of management, predominate. Good human resource management is also a key factor. 'Learning organizations', which capitalize on improvements and rigorously apply them to every possible area of the organization, also tend to succeed. Other vital factors include:

■ selecting the right TQM approach

■ committing sufficient time and other resources to the programme

■ balancing the use of technical and people skills

■ the ability to apply, consolidate and extend practical improvements to every relevant part of the organization

Notes

1 Adapted from *The Improvement Process*, by H. J. Harrington (1987), p. 40.

2 *Fortune*, 'The Race to Quality Improvement' (1989), p. 53.

3 *The Improvement Process* (1987), p. 46.

4 *Managing Change*, by Philip Sadler, Kogan Page (1995).

5 *Business Process Improvement*, by H. J. Harrington, McGraw-Hill (1991), p. 249.

6 *Fortune* (1989), p. 9.

Section 2 Quality assessment and planning

Introduction

The purpose of this section of the workbook is to give you some practical guidance in the pre-planning and planning stages of introducing TQM, which were identified in the previous section. It contains activities which allow you to analyse your own organization in terms of its customer expectations and key success factors. This will enable you to tailor a definition of quality for your own enterprise.

You will continue by assessing several factors which will help you to determine whether pursuing Total Quality Management is right for your organization. These factors include how well you are attaining your own quality standards at the moment, and the attitudes to quality currently prevailing in your organization.

Assuming you have decided to pursue a quality improvement programme, you will go on to consider the areas in your organization where piloting a TQM test programme would be most fruitful. You will identify an area where quality could be significantly improved, on the one hand, and where results would be most visible and dramatic (and success most likely), on the other. Selecting a test site for a pilot TQM initiative is a matter of finding an area where there is conjunction between all these factors.

Finally, advice and activities are provided to help you begin the process of planning and resourcing a TQM initiative. This includes guidance on determining goals, milestones and success criteria, and on identifying and costing resources for the initiative.

WHERE THIS SECTION FITS

Now that you have an overview of the process of introducing a TQM initiative, you are ready to begin the early stages of pre-planning and planning. Pre-planning concerns itself with customizing a definition of quality for your organization, and assessing both the need for quality improvements and the attitudes to quality. Once you have decided to pursue a quality initiative, planning encompasses a number of practical issues such as appointing change agents, selecting an appropriate TQM route, and identifying training needs.

No one individual can plan a TQM initiative single-handedly. Assessment and planning are complicated procedures, and you will need more than this workbook to steer you through them. It is likely that if your pre-planning activities lead to a decision to start planning, you will appoint a full-time internal quality co-ordinator who will be assisted by an external management consultancy. This section, along with the rest of the workbook, can give you a good grounding in the issues you and the rest of the quality planning team will need to address. It provides you with an overview and checklists on practical issues to research, consider, and ultimately devise action plans for.

Defining quality for your organization

You have already identified your customers' expectations in Activity 1. The following activity will help you begin to translate these expectations into the critical success factors you will use to measure and improve quality in your particular organization. (For our purposes here, we are considering external customers, who can generally be defined as the people who buy your products or services. In certain organizations (for example public service institutions), there can be several categories of customer, sometimes with conflicting demands. If this is the case in your organization, senior management will need to prioritize which are the most important customers to focus on in a quality initiative.)

Return to Activity 1 (p. 3), to recall your customers' expectations. Now derive your organization's critical success factors from these expectations. This is a matter of considering what your customers want and working out what it means to your organization to be able to deliver it. For example, the customers of a shoe shop might want:

- to buy shoes immediately, without being told they'll have to wait for a stock delivery
- low prices
- good customer service

From the shop's point of view, these customer expectations translate into the following critical success factors.

Customer expectation	→	**Critical success factor**
■ immediate purchase	→	■ holding enough stock to satisfy demand
■ low prices	→	■ efficient operations
■ customer service	→	■ trained staff

Now complete the following table for your own organization. After you have filled in the expectations of your customers and the related critical success factors, prioritize the critical success factors in terms of importance.

Customer expectation	→	**Critical success factor**	**Priority**
■	→	■	
■	→	■	
■	→	■	
■	→	■	
■	→	■	

FEEDBACK

Your ability to deliver quality to your customers depends on your organization's ability to achieve these critical success factors efficiently and effectively.

Profiling quality in your organization

Knowing your critical success factors can help you assess how well quality is currently achieved, and the extent to which improving quality is a strategic policy in your organization. The following two activities will help you start thinking about these issues.

In the light of your most recent customer satisfaction information, answer the following questions.

1   How well do we meet our customers' expectations? What is the total number of complaints, returns, refunds, customer defections, and so on, per 100 (or 1000 or 10 000) sales or customer contacts?

2   What is the cost of this level of customer dissatisfaction? For example, what proportion of sales or profit does it represent?

3   How well do our competitors (or similar organizations) score in this area?

FEEDBACK

If you do not know the answers to these questions, you will need to obtain them before you can seriously consider the practicalities of launching a TQM initiative. This sort of quantifiable data is one of the foundations of a viable Total Quality approach.

On the issue of benchmarking (question 3), it is likely that information about direct rivals' performances will be available only in the most sophisticated and progressive markets. However, organizations in similar but not directly competitive markets (for example, aircraft manufacturers and ship-builders, or hotels and travel agencies) might arrange to share benchmarking information in a mutually advantageous way. Other sources of benchmarking information include:

- trade associations
- financial reports
- market research
- reports in the media, including newspaper and magazine articles
- the British Quality Foundation, whose address is given after the Recommended Reading list

ACTIVITY 10

The following checklist will help you begin to assess where your organization has travelled on the path to quality, and the level of commitment in your organization to a conscious quality strategy.

	Yes	No
1 Do we have written quality standards?	❏	❏
2 Do we have a quality manual?	❏	❏
3 Do we have a quality assurance department?	❏	❏
4 Do we have accreditation, or are we seeking accreditation, for BS 5750 or ISO 9000?	❏	❏
5 Is quality improvement a conscious strategic objective?	❏	❏
6 Is it enshrined in our mission statement, our statement of principles, and high-level corporate goals?	❏	❏
7 If so, have these been translated into measurable tactical and operational goals?	❏	❏
8 If so, is everyone in the organization aware of the overall corporate quality objectives and of how these translate into the quality standards and goals of their own department?	❏	❏

FEEDBACK

It may be unlikely that you answered yes to all of these questions. Even if you have, however, your organization may not have translated this commitment to quality into a fully efficient operation consistently delivering your own particular version of zero defects. The checklist can give you some idea of where your organization has travelled on the 'journey to quality'. Knowing this can help you identify the requirements of the publicity campaign, cultural change programme and training initiative needed in your Total Quality programme.

Activity 9 has indicated the current level of quality in your organization (measured in terms of customer satisfaction). Activity 10 has indicated where your organization is now in terms of its practice and attitudes to quality. The next activity helps you evaluate the need and the motivation to improve your quality position, and assess whether the climate in your organization is favourable to a quality initiative.

ACTIVITY 11

1 Are your poor-quality costs high?

2 Is there truly the will among senior management to institute fundamental change to achieve quality, considering all the risks, costs and disadvantages of TQM as described in Section 1?

3 Is morale, trust and the general culture of your organization conducive to the launch of a quality programme?

FEEDBACK

You may feel that you need more information before making a decision about any of these questions. If so, try to obtain as much evidence as possible. You will also be seeking information and opinions on these issues from your management colleagues.

If you are confident that your poor-quality costs are too high, and that top management are whole-heartedly prepared to lead and support a Total Quality initiative, you may want to proceed to the next stage of pre-planning. (An optimal organizational culture is not an absolute prerequisite to launching a quality programme, but if it is not optimal, changing the culture will need to become a top priority in your TQM programme.)

The final stage of pre-planning involves inviting input from the managers of all the other departments of the organization, and discussing their responses. At this stage, one expert, John Macdonald, recommends a six-step programme to systematically gather further input from appropriate colleagues.[1]

1 Convene the heads of all departments for a presentation on TQM and its relevance to your organization.
2 Ask each department head to consider the questions in Activities 1 to 4, and their possible relevance in their departments.
3 Ask them to discuss with their subordinates the causes and levels of possible poor-quality costs in their department, ensuring that it is understood that these may involve circumstances outside their control, and that no one is seeking to assign blame.
4 The following week, collect their findings by interviewing each head of department.

5   Ask the finance department to cost the poor-quality costs identified.

6   Invite the heads of department to a meeting where the findings are presented.

On the basis of these findings and the discussions that follow, the senior management of the organization will need to decide whether to commit the resources to continue planning a TQM programme.

Starting to plan

THE PLANNING TEAM

If the organization does decide to plan in earnest for a TQM initiative, a TQM planning and management team will need to be appointed. The members of the team should be drawn from the existing management team, with senior departmental managers overseen by a steering committee of top managers (sometimes called a quality council). The planning team should be carefully selected to include managers with good technical abilities and people skills. TQM enthusiasts should be balanced by the inclusion of a few known sceptics, to keep the process grounded in reality. The team should be headed by an internal quality co-ordinator, who will act as the main change agent inside the organization. This individual will be assisted, at all levels, as needed, by various facilitators and specialists. Figure 6 illustrates the ideal structure.

Ultimately the management of quality will be fully integrated into the normal responsibilities of both managers and other employees in the organization. During the planning and implementation phases, however, the quality management team will need to be active in overseeing and driving the quality initiative.

There are three major decisions that the planning team will need to make in the early stages of planning:

■   which TQM model to follow

■   which management consultancy to use

■   whether to launch the quality programme throughout the entire organization all at once, or to pilot it in one department or area first

The first two decisions might be interdependent. Some consultants are more experienced in using one model rather than another; whereas others might use a more integrated approach, drawing on the various methods employed by several of the major quality gurus.

The major gurus are:

- W. Edwards Deming
- Joseph Moses Juran
- Philip Crosby
- Kaoru Ishikawa

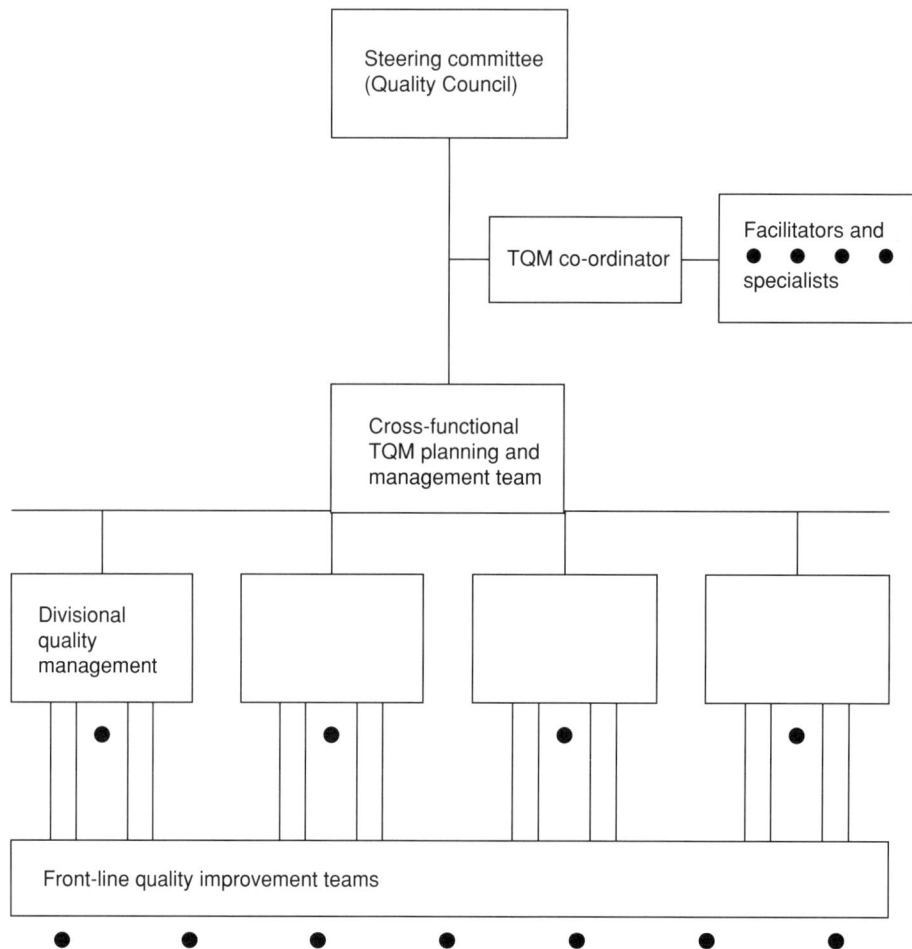

Figure 6   The structure of a TQM management team

The differences between these gurus are too complicated to outline here, but you can find out more about their approaches from the Appendix and from the books mentioned in the Recommended Reading list. Your management consultants can also provide advice about the practical applications of their ideas in real organizations.

ACTIVITY 12

Note down the major points you would ask management consultants to address in a tender bid.

FEEDBACK

Your list probably includes:

- cost
- schedule
- a detailed outline of their recommended approach
- evidence of ability to deliver guidance and training on both technical elements and interpersonal skills
- CVs of key personnel
- names of satisfied clients and other evidence of successful work in organizations such as yours

BIG BANG OR STEP-BY-STEP?

The planning team, guided by the steering committee, must also must decide how to approach TQM in their own organization. There are two ways of introducing Total Quality Management into an organization:

- the Big Bang approach
- the incremental approach

The Big Bang method seeks to introduce TQM throughout the entire organization at once. Months or even years may be spent in planning, preparing for and publicizing the event, but the intention is to 'go live' at a particular moment on a particular day.

The advantage of the Big Bang approach is that it is dramatic and signals a total commitment to TQM and an expectation that every employee will enact quality. Its disadvantages are that it is costly, requires a lot of energy from everyone in the organization and demands superb leadership. It is a very public statement, which offers the organization no opportunity to backtrack or learn from mistakes. Employees may respond sceptically to the hype and view it as just another excuse to push people even harder. Morale can be seriously damaged if the initiative suffers teething troubles (as is often the case).

You may be justified in thinking that the disadvantages of the Big Bang approach outweigh its advantages. Certainly one experienced management consultant has remarked, 'The Big Bang doesn't work in the UK.' Perhaps this is because, in the current UK business climate, downsizing and redundancies are justifiably feared, and TQM programmes are often instituted as cost-cutting exercises.

The incremental approach relies on introducing TQM gradually, using a carefully designed pilot programme to achieve early success, boost morale, and 'sell' TQM to the rest of the organization. Its advantages include cost effectiveness, lower risk, and the fact that it allows the organization to sort out teething troubles in private, before going public. Managed effectively, it delivers a relevant, in-house success to convert the sceptical and provide some drive and enthusiasm for implementing the programme in the rest of the organization.

Its disadvantages include its potential to send the wrong messages to the organization about quality:

- that quality can be hived off in certain elite departments
- that quality is seen as 'something other people do'

Without determined effort, there is also a risk that even a successful pilot programme could lose its impetus before reaching the entire organization.

ACTIVITY 13

Which approach seems best for your organization: the Big Bang or the incremental approach? Note down the most important criteria in your organization for making this decision.

FEEDBACK

Each organization, guided by internal and consultant change agents, must decide whether the Big Bang or the incremental approach is most likely to deliver optimal results. For the purposes of this section, it is assumed that you will follow the incremental approach in starting to plan a pilot programme. However, the skills and tasks necessary to plan an initiative on any scale are basically the same, with the activities associated with larger, complex projects broken down into smaller subprocesses.

IDENTIFYING A STARTING POINT

If the incremental approach is selected, the planning team has to identify the area or department of the organization in which to pilot TQM. The pilot area should be one which has the highest potential to deliver a dramatic success in terms of quantifiable quality improvement, and should have some or all of the following characteristics:

- a real need for quality improvements
- the potential to deliver significant improvements with a demonstrable impact on the bottom line
- the potential to generate solutions which may be carried into other areas or locations in the organization
- a high-profile, mainstream position in the organization's process chain
- demanding technical processes
- a skilled, well-trained workforce
- reasonably high morale
- employees with experience of teamwork and group problem solving (or at least the potential to learn these)
- good managers, with excellent leadership and people management skills
- good relationships between managers and informal leaders

In any case, the incremental approach should not be piloted in the quality assurance department, as this sends the message that the organization is willing to 'hive off' quality into a separate department.

ACTIVITY 14   A5

What section or area of your organization do you feel is the best candidate for a pilot TQM programme? Justify your decision as fully as possible.

IDENTIFYING GOALS AND PLANNING FOR THEM

Once the pilot area has been chosen, the planning team concentrates on establishing the goals the quality initiative will work toward. These goals should mesh with, reinforce and drive forward the organization's overall strategic goals. The quality goals should be constructed to ensure that they do not cause suboptimization in other parts of the process. For example, a process improvement in the pilot area should not be achieved at the expense of quality in any other link in the process chain. An improvement only qualifies as a Total Quality improvement if everybody wins by it.

Milestones are interim achievements along the way toward full attainment of the overall goals. Goals are long-term objectives (say, over a year or longer). Milestones focus on key progress markers in the shorter term. (An example of a milestone would be the first quality circle meeting of a particular workteam.) Planning in milestones, and celebrating and publicizing them as they are reached, is an important aspect of good planning.

In practice the planning team will establish a number of the goals and milestones in conjunction with the managers and employees of the pilot programme. Planners should expect to do a great deal of active listening. One of the key dimensions by which the initiative will be judged is the extent to which employees 'own' the quality improvements, and a vital element to ensuring this is to invite and act on their input. Overall, the test of an effective programme is that employees not only achieve quality improvements but feel excited and proud of their achievements, and strongly motivated to carry them on.

Success criteria will let you know when (and how well) the pilot programme has succeeded in attaining the quality goals. In determining success criteria, the planning team must cover the following areas:

- quantifiable and financially measurable data about the effect of the pilot programme on the department's output and on the organization overall
- an assessment of employee morale and teamwork based on employee interviews
- feedback from all internal customers to the output of the pilot area

A viable quality plan will also specify how the goals will be met. It should identify and schedule the detailed steps by which the milestones and objectives will be achieved. In general, such plans must consider the following issues:

- identifying and delivering training in interpersonal skills
- identifying and delivering training in problem-solving and process-improvement skills
- expert help in process analysis
- facilitation of group-working methods
- the methods for reviewing and auditing progress in the pilot programme

ACTIVITY 15

What are some of the possible goals, milestones and success criteria for a pilot programme in your organization?

Identifying resources

Part of the detailed planning of the pilot programme involves identifying and costing necessary resources. The planning team will need to make estimates about the cost of:

- external consultants
- customer satisfaction research
- process analysis
- supplier liaison, training or renegotiation
- training at all levels
- down-time, including managers' and planning team time

You will find more detailed information about training issues in Section 4, which focuses on people management issues and skills, and in Section 5, which focuses on technical issues and skills. You will need to read these sections before tackling a full-scale costing exercise.

ACTIVITY 16

After you have gathered enough information, you might like to use the following worksheet as the starting point for your costing exercise. Add in any specific additional cost areas which relate to your organization's pilot programme.

Pilot quality programme cost estimates

1 We estimate that costs for external management consultants will be: £_____

2 We estimate that costs for customer satisfaction research will be: £_____

3 We estimate that process analysis costs will be:

   ■ process analysis expert's consultancy fees: £_____

   ■ down time: _____ worker days at an average of £_____ per day, giving a cost of: £_____

   ■ related managerial time: _____ manager days at an average of £_____ per day, giving a cost of: £_____

   ■ related equipment or materials costs: £_____

Total process analysis costs: £_____

4 We estimate that costs for supplier liaison, training or renegotiation will be: £_____

   ■ related equipment or materials costs: £_____

   ■ other related costs (transportation, hospitality, etc.): £_____

   ■ Total supplier costs: £_____

5 We estimate that training costs will be:

   ■ managers' soft skills training:

      _____ trainer days at an average of £_____ per day: £_____

      _____ manager days at an average of £_____ per day £_____

   ■ managers' technical skills training:

   ■ trainer days at an average of £_____ per day: £_____

      _____ manager days at an average of £_____ per day: £_____

   ■ employees' soft skills training:

      _____ trainer days at an average of £_____ per day: £_____

      _____ manager days at an average of £_____ per day: £_____

   ■ employees' technical skills training:

      _____ trainer days at an average of £_____ per day: £_____

      _____ manager days at an average of £_____ per day: £_____

   ■ costs of training materials or equipment: £_____

Total training costs: £_____

6 We estimate that facilitation costs for quality group meetings will be: £_____

7 We estimate that costs for planning team time will be: _____ planner days at an average of £_____ per day, giving a cost of: £_____

8 Other costs (itemize): £_____

Total estimated cost: £_____

The following activity helps you to consolidate your learning in this section.

ACTIVITY 17

1 Explain how you would derive an organization's critical success factors from its customers' expectations.

2 What benefit is there in determining your organization's current position on the path to quality?

3 How can benchmarking help you in planning a quality initiative?

4 Give three types of information you will need to know in order to determine the 'quality profile' of your organization.

5 How would you go about involving departmental heads throughout your organization in assessing quality issues?

6 At what stage does top management have sufficient information to make a decision about launching a quality initiative?

7 Briefly outline the membership of the TQM planning team.

8 What three initial major decisions will the planning team need to make?

9 What are the relative advantages and disadvantages of the Big Bang and incremental approaches?

10 What issues must be considered when setting success criteria for a pilot TQM initiative?

11 Name five or six general areas of activity which must be scheduled, resourced and costed in planning a TQM initiative.

FEEDBACK

If you had difficulties with any question in the previous activity, refresh your memory by re-reading the relevant section. Or you might find it useful to discuss the issue with a colleague.

Summary

- The pre-planning stage of a Total Quality initiative is concerned with assessing both the need for quality improvement and the attitude to quality within your organization. From your knowledge of customer expectations, it is possible to derive the quality-related critical success factors for your enterprise. Actual performance, and customer reactions, can indicate how well these factors are being addressed in your current operations.

- Once you have some idea of how well you are doing, you can analyse the existing attitudes toward quality in your organization to find out where your organization is on the path to quality and how much further you need to travel. This is a matter of gathering information and of inviting input from your colleagues. At this stage, the heads of all departments will need to become involved in more detailed quality audits for their sections. As a result of this information- and opinion-gathering exercise, top management will decide whether to commit resources to planning a Total Quality initiative.

- If the planning stage is green lighted, a planning team will need to be appointed. This usually consists of senior managers from each department, overseen by a steering committee of top managers and led by an internal quality co-ordinator who is the main change agent inside the organization. At this stage, the team will probably decide to buy in the services of management consultants experienced in implementing Total Quality initiatives. Choosing consultants will be one of the major decisions the planning team makes.

■ They will also have to decide which of the several TQM methods to follow, and whether to adopt a Big Bang or incremental approach. The planning tasks and skills are essentially the same for both approaches. If the incremental approach is selected, the planners will need to identify the department or section of the organization where a quality initiative is likely to be most rewarding.

■ The planning team, in consultation with the managers and employees of the department, identifies the initiative's intended goals, milestones and criteria for success. Planning is a matter of developing detailed procedures and schedules for both the people management issues and the technical issues on which Total Quality Management depends. Resources for the programme must also be identified and costed. Finally, the team must decide how the initiative is to be monitored, reviewed and evaluated.

Note

1 Adapted from *Understanding TQM in a Week*, by John Macdonald, Headway/Institute of Management (1993), pp. 28–9.

Section 3
Communicating and gaining commitment

Introduction

In this section of the workbook, you will look at the issues of communicating and gaining commitment for a TQM initiative. The section is in two parts:

- the first part focuses on issues of organizational culture
- the second part gives you guidance on how to devise a communication plan for a TQM programme in your organization

One of the most important aspects of gaining commitment is fostering an organizational culture which can sustain and nourish Total Quality Management. The first part of this section briefly reviews some definitions and characteristics of organizational culture, then describes the type of organizational culture which is most favourable to TQM. You then have an opportunity to analyse your own organizational culture. The discussion ends by outlining some approaches for modifying organizational culture to make it more favourable to a TQM programme.

The second part of the section discusses some approaches for devising a plan to communicate and publicize an upcoming TQM initiative. It examines the issue of resistance to change and suggests some measures which can minimize such resistance. One of the most important measures is a proactive communication strategy which builds up both enthusiasm and understanding of the quality process. A well-constructed communication programme can convince employees of the benefits of a quality initiative for themselves, the customers and the organization as a whole.

WHERE THIS SECTION FITS

TQM is a holistic approach which relies on every member of an organization working toward a shared vision. Every member of the organization must understand the quality-focused approach and the objectives of the TQM initiative in their workplace, and be committed to them.

One extremely important dimension of the planning process is analysing the organizational environment to determine the character and extent of any necessary cultural changes. Making such necessary changes is a critical part of gaining commitment to the TQM initiative.

The TQM management team will also need to formulate and carry out a plan for communicating and gaining commitment for the quality initiative. The cultural and communication aspects of a TQM programme are closely linked. The sensitive handling of these interdependent aspects is a prerequisite for success in any quality initiative.

Culture

As you saw in Section 1, one of the reasons a Total Quality Management initiative can founder is because it is introduced into an organization with an unfavourable culture. The shift to Total Quality Management represents a radical change for any organization. The word 'radical' means 'from the roots up'. The roots of a TQM programme are embedded in, and nourished by, the soil of organizational environment. And just as it would be unproductive to plant a valuable plant in the wrong type of soil, so it would be ill-advised to introduce TQM into an organization with an antithetical culture. Such attempts are doomed to failure.

This is not to say that organizational culture must be perfectly congenial before TQM is even envisaged. As we noted earlier, it is possible to change an organization's culture as part of a TQM initiative – and in fact a certain amount of cultural change is inevitable. It is important that, in the early stages of the planning process, an organization's senior management, aided by its TQM management team, understand:

- the character of the organizational culture
- the aspects of the culture that need to change
- the extent of cultural change needed
- management's responsibility to initiate and see through these changes – starting with putting its own house in order

The concept of organizational culture has become a familiar one in the past two decades. One well-known definition describes it as 'the commonly shared beliefs, values and characteristic patterns of behaviour that exist within an organisation'.[1] Perhaps the best, and most commonly known definition of organizational culture, however, is simply 'the way we do things around here'.[2] Although management texts often differentiate between organizational culture and other aspects of the organizational environment such as structure, policy and so on, for our purposes in this section, we can use the terms 'culture' and 'environment' interchangeably.

It is useful to remember the four basic types of organizational culture outlined by R. Harrison (and further popularized by Charles Handy):

- **power-oriented: characterized by its emphasis on the personal, often autocratic, power of its leader, and the control that powerful people in the organization try to exercise over subordinates**
- **role-oriented: characterized by its emphasis on hierarchy and status, and its rule-dominated, bureaucratic procedures**
- **task-oriented: characterized by its often project-based focus and its emphasis on team work and getting the job done**
- **people-oriented: characterized by its egalitarianism and its emphasis on the needs and self-fulfilment of its members**

ACTIVITY 18

Which of these types of culture does your organization most resemble?

With the exception of people-oriented culture (which tends to be found only in families, communes and similar groups), any of these cultures may be found in today's business or public service organizations. It is likely that either role-oriented or task-oriented cultures are more favourable to Total Quality Management initiatives than power cultures, which are unlikely to encourage the necessary collaboration, information-sharing and empowerment.

Charles Handy has depicted role cultures as classical temples underpinned by a number of separate, 'functional' columns, with only the top management hierarchy spanning the entire breadth of the organization. Organizations with such an emphasis on vertical relationships and the autonomy of separate functions are likely to have mutually hostile 'departmental fortresses' and entrenched, rigid systems for doing things. All these factors tend to create impediments to the smooth flow of processes 'horizontally' through the organization.

Task cultures have been depicted as webs or nets. With their emphasis on corporate goals, horizontal as well as vertical communications, and teamwork, task cultures have some of the features necessary to support TQM. Care must be taken, however, to ensure that project teams are able to look outside their own particular cell of the web. Teams must not become so cohesive and inwardly focused that they are unaware of their internal customers in the process chain, and of other colleagues in the rest of the organization.

QUALITY-ORIENTED CULTURE

Total Quality organizations tend to develop a fifth type of organizational culture: quality-oriented culture. This culture is based on the organization's mission and on the guiding principles and values that underpin it: for example showing respect and fairness toward all employees, and responsibility toward internal and external customers, the wider community, and the environment.

Quality cultures also have characteristically participative management and leadership styles. Management ensures that a good flow of communications is maintained, changing systems and structures where necessary to facilitate this. It also recognizes that communication entails listening as well as talking. In the process of establishing good communications, departmental fortresses are dismantled, and hostility and competitiveness are replaced with co-operation.

An important part of collaborative management is a deliberate human resources policy of empowerment. Empowerment has become something of a management buzz word in the past decade, but true empowerment is based on solid principles and good common sense. It seeks to release, develop, use and reward the full potential of every employee. This involves consulting with, training and developing employees, and breaking down long-standing distinctions between 'chiefs' and 'Indians', between thinkers and doers.

This sounds radical and it is. It is also a vital prerequisite for a successful TQM programme. In order to work, this new style of employee relations must begin with top management and flow downward through each management level in what Harrington calls the 'waterfall effect', 'wash[ing] each level of management clean of its old, bad habits before it touches the next lower level of management or employees.'[3] This requires systematic training for all levels of management, not just for well-meaning but out-of-touch upper and middle management, but for front-line managers and supervisors too.

The rewards of empowerment include a workforce with higher self-esteem and morale, better labour relations, and increases in creativity and innovation, in problem solving and problem prevention. All this adds up to lower poor-quality costs and a higher return on investment in wages, always a significant expenditure in any organization. It also makes the quality initiative meaningful and rewarding for all members of the organization, who will realize that the move to Total Quality brings with it a better quality of life in the workplace.

ACTIVITY 19

Analyse your organization's culture using the form below. Rate your organization on the following issues on a scale from one to five, with one representing the lowest and five the highest rating. Unless indicated otherwise, the term 'employee' refers to all members of the organization at all levels.

	1	2	3	4	5
Customer focus To what extent are employees aware of and responsible to their internal customers?					
To what extent are employees aware of and responsible to their external customers?					
Quality focus					
How serious is management about quality?					
How serious are non-managerial employees about quality?					
Morale To what extent do employees feel valued, and that their contribution makes a difference to the organization?					
To what extent do employees feel that they are using their full potential and challenging their abilities at work?					
What rate of employee turnover does the organization have? (1 = high; 5 = low)					
Communication How effective are the vertical channels of communication in the organization?					
How effective are the horizontal channels of communication in the organization?					
Are managers at all levels aware of their subordinates' problems and concerns?					
Do managers at all levels share information with their subordinates?					

	1	2	3	4	5
Participative management What level of delegation, with adequate support, is there in the organization?					
To what extent do managers share resources, responsibility and credit with subordinates?					
What level of training and development do employees at all levels receive?					
What is the overall level of trust between managers and subordinates?					
Teamwork How well do individuals work together?					
How well do departments work together?					
To what extent is there a collaborative ethic throughout the organization?					

FEEDBACK

This activity has given you the opportunity to examine the environment in your organization. It may have highlighted the fact that yours is already a 'quality culture'. Or it may have thrown into relief certain specific areas which need modifying, or indicated a more generalized shortfall between your organization and the ideal 'quality-oriented culture'.

Planning for cultural change

If there are aspects of the environment in need of improvement, these must be addressed in a holistic way, by introducing structural and systems-based changes, if necessary, rather than simply announcing a 'cultural revolution' unsupported by specific back-up measures.

Cultural change must start at the top, with the people who have the most power and responsibility: senior executives and management. Management must 'walk their talk': plan change, make it happen, and be seen to make it happen, before the workforce can be expected to take a quality initiative seriously. Cultural change must be related to strategic goals and to the organization's overarching principles.

MORALE

Whether or not the TQM management team feels it needs more information about employee morale, a survey of all employees should be conducted. This serves the threefold purpose of:

- gathering accurate information
- consulting directly and openly with employees
- helping to communicate details of the quality initiative to the workforce

The organization should not consider conducting such a survey, however, unless it is prepared to share the results with the workforce and undertake corrective action if the survey shows morale to be low. Employees' anonymity should be guaranteed and the organization should make it clear, at the time of distributing questionnaires, when and how feedback on the survey will be given to each department. Feedback, especially in small departments, should be sensitively handled to ensure anonymity and preserve everyone's dignity.

A sample employee morale questionnaire is shown in Figure 7.

It should be emphasized that the morale survey is only the beginning of a consultative process between management and the rest of the workforce, the aim of which is to increase quality throughout the organization. This entails not only better quality for internal and external customers, but an improvement in the quality of job satisfaction for employees at all levels. Management must not deceive themselves or the workforce about this. Without a full commitment and full follow-through to this level of collaboration, Total Quality Management will not succeed.

1 How would you describe your overall level of satisfaction with the organization?
   a completely dissatisfied
   b very dissatisfied
   c moderate
   d reasonably satisfied
   e very satisfied
2 How well do you like your job?
   a not at all
   b not much
   c feel neutral
   d like it farily well
   e enjoy it a lot
3 To what extent do you feel the organization is making full use of your skills
   a not at all
   b not much
   c sometimes
   d usually
   e most of the time
4 To what extent do you feel that enjoyable, effective teamwork is promoted in the
   organization?
   a not at all
   b not much
   c sometimes
   d usually
   e most of the time
5 To what extent do you feel your line manager shares information with you and allows you
   to discuss work-related problems with him or her?
   a not at all
   b not much
   c sometimes
   d usually
   e most of the time
6 To what extent do you think things need improvement or could operate better in your
   department or work group?
   a things are a shambles
   b things need a lot of improvement
   c some things need improvement
   d things usually work well
   e things work well most of the time
7 What level of trust and confidence do you have in your manager?
   a none at all
   b very little
   c some
   d quite a bit
   e a lot
8 What seems to be management's greatest concern?
   a cost
   b quality
   c schedules
9 What seems to be management's least concern?
   a cost
   b quality
   c schedules

Figure 7   A sample employee morale questionnaire.[4]

ACTIVITY 20   A5, F1, F3

This activity will help you begin to plan for cultural change. On the following action plan, identify the most pressing cultural change needed in your organization, break it down into separate tasks, and note down some ways in which they could be achieved. Use separate copies of the action plan for each major cultural change needed. If you are planning a TQM programme in earnest, your colleagues and management consultants should help with this exercise.

Action plan for cultural change

The most pressing cultural change needed in our organization is:

This can be broken down into the following tasks:

Ways of starting to achieve these are:

Desired result	Action/s needed	By whom	By when

FEEDBACK

You may find that the following list helps you to identify your organization's needs (or you may find it more helpful to state them in your own words).

Necessary cultural changes might include:

■ improving the organization's customer focus for either internal or external customers
■ communicating to employees a better understanding of and commitment to quality principles
■ empowering managers to empower their subordinates
■ improving morale
■ increasing trust between different parts of the organization
■ widening and improving communication structures and habits
■ dismantling cultural barriers between thinkers and doers
■ dismantling departmental fortresses
■ giving training and development a higher priority

Confronting and defusing resistance

It would be unrealistic to expect that a fundamental change programme such as TQM could be introduced into an organization without meeting a certain amount of resistance. It is natural for people to resist change in their working environment. Employees at all levels may oppose change for a variety of reasons, including:

■ fear of redundancy or loss of financial benefits
■ fear of worsening working conditions, with possible consequences for their private lives
■ fear of failure to master new, unfamiliar working practices and skills
■ insecurity over possible loss of status
■ suspicion about new ideas and their workability
■ lack of energy or motivation to learn new skills
■ fear of management's hidden motives, such as job cuts or plant closures
■ fear of losing control
■ fear of workteams and other informal social groups being broken up

H. J. Harrington's observations of American quality initiatives in the 1980s indicated that the major resistance to quality programmes came not from the shop floor but from middle and front-line managers. This was the group which felt it had most to lose and least to gain from the pervasive changes that Total Quality Management requires. Whether this is true in British organizations is unclear, but certainly every TQM implementation plan must include detailed provision for 'marketing' the initiative to all groups, particularly concentrating on those whose resistance is believed to be strongest.

Where do you think resistance to a quality initiative would be strongest in your organization?

What do you foresee as the major reasons for this resistance?

What measures do you think would be most effective in defusing the potential resistance?

Defusing resistance is a matter of allowing employees to discuss reservations and misgivings openly, without allowing the dialogue to become adversarial. Patience, persuasion and a positive attitude are required for this, as well as a well-thought-out programme of training. In addition, it is important to acknowledge – and offer employees support for – the stress which can be generated by change in the workplace.

A programme to address resistance to change is likely to require the services of excellent human resource specialists. Your organization may have these in-house, your management consultants may have such specialists on their team, or they may be able to help you find such specialists elsewhere. If the HR tasks are outsourced, however, it is vital that relevant departments and managers within the organization are closely involved in the process, so that it is not seen as an externally imposed (and therefore optional) programme.

Harrington recommends that a 'no redundancies' policy is vital to ensure workforce support for a TQM initiative. If an organization's management is unable to give such an assurance, any job cutting must be handled according to best practice in human resource management, and in a way which communicates that the organization is operating with fairness and compassion.

The communication strategy

An organization introducing a Total Quality initiative can minimize resistance to change by constructing a careful strategy for informing employees about the programme. A publicity and 'marketing' strategy should be fully integrated with the related processes of consultation with, and training of, employees at all levels. Involving all members of the organization in a change programme is one of the key factors in achieving change successfully.

Another key aspect is allowing sufficient time for the change initiative. The communication and consultation programme must be allocated sufficient time. Initiating change takes time: it requires time to consult with employees, to build up trust, and to consolidate new skills. The 'waterfall effect' takes time, as does building up a critical mass of trained managers and employees to take the TQM initiative forward. Effective publicity measures should precede and accompany each new stage of the initiative. Equally important, the organization should make sure that key milestones and successes are publicized and celebrated. The communications strategy should seek to win hearts as well as minds, uplift morale and generally create an organizational esprit de corps.

It is also important that the organization persevere in the communication process. Publicity and information should be given repeatedly during the communication programme, and in a variety of media. It takes time for messages to filter through to the entire workforce, and different individuals will pay attention to different media. The various types of media that could be used include:

- articles in the organization's staff newspaper
- a special 'Quality' edition of the newspaper
- posters
- leaflets
- personal letters to each employee
- special bulletin boards dedicated to the quality initiative
- video
- in-house radio broadcasts (if feasible)
- company-wide meetings (if size and location permits)
- briefings to individual departments or work groups

ACTIVITY 22

What combination of these (or other) methods of communication would best suit a communication programme in your organization?

Of course, training also counts as a key element in communicating and gaining acceptance for a Total Quality initiative. (Training is discussed further in Section 4.) Front-line workers will be trained by their supervisors or line managers, who will also be the key people in the consultation process. The involvement of supervisors and line managers is a vital aspect in gaining commitment to a TQM programme and integrating it into the fundamental practices of departments and work groups.

Communication programmes are most effective if the organization is able to share the vision of the change agents, and help employees to imagine the better future for themselves and the organization after the change has been achieved. The organization should seek to generate commitment to the initiative by informing employees at all levels about:

- what's in it for **them**
- what's in it for the **customers**
- what's in it for the **organization**

The process of gaining commitment will be more successful if the organization frankly and honestly acknowledges the difficulties and stresses that any change programme can bring about. The stress of change can be limited and made manageable if the organization recognizes that the change may cause employees difficulties, encourages employees to discuss their concerns, listens carefully, and takes measures, such as providing stress counselling, to help minimize problems. Figure 8 illustrates a sample timetable for communicating a TQM programme.

	Week commencing	Activity	Communication event	People involved
Pre-planning	10 February	Initial research		planners
	24 February	Start of quality research in each department	TQM presentation	planners senior management heads of departments
	31 March	Results of departmental research	Meeting presenting research findings	planners senior management heads of departments
	14 April	Decisions to proceed to planning of pilot		senior management (Quality Council)
Planning pilot	19 May	Consultation/decision to pilot TQM in Engineering Dept	Consultation with managers and front-line workers	planners all of Engineering Dept
	26 May	Planning of pilot continuing	Special Quality Boards installed; 'tantalizer' posters put up	all areas of organizations, especially Engineering Dept
	9 June	Meeting do discuss TQM	Briefing on TQM by planners and Engineering managers	planners Engineering Dept
	30 June	Pilot planning continues	'Stop Press' article in company newsletter about TQM pilot: 'Guess what's happening in Engineering?'	all Employees
Implementation of pilot	7 July and throughout summer	Training of Engineering employees in 'soft' and 'hard' skills	Series of 'TQM' Success Stories' posters on Quality Bulletin Boards continues	all departments especially Engineering
	21 July	Pilot implementation begins	Personal letters from senior managers to Engineering employees in pay packets	senior managers Engineering employees
Pilot review	3 November	Review of pilot	Fill-page story in company newsletter about results and success of pilot	all employees
Planning	5 January	Planning to implement TQM in entire organization	Special Quality Edition Newsletter, announcing company-wide programme plans	all departments

Figure 8   A sample timetable for communicating a TQM programme

	Week commencing	Activity	Communication event	People involved
Organization-wide initiative	19 January	Planning continues	Employee morale survey	all departments
	2 February	Planning continues	Feedbacks of results of morale surveys in each department	all departments
	16 February	Planning conditions	Briefing on TQM and what it means for each department	managers and front-line workers in all departments
	9 March	Planning continues	Video of training and process analysis in Engineering pilot programme	managers and front-line workers in all departments
Implementation	23 March	Preparation for launch of implementation phase	Personal letters from senior managers to all employees in pay packets	senior managers all employees
	30 March	Implementation begins	Training in 'hard' and 'soft' skills for all employees	all employees
	30 March to 23 November	Implementation continues	Regular updates in newsletter about TQM in various departments and stories about successes; awards, presentations and celebrations to mark milestones and successes	all employees
Review	30 November	Review phase begins	Posters, leaflets and Special Edition of newsletter, all detailing the results and benefits of TQM initatives for the employees, the company and its customers	all employees

Figure 8 *(Continued)*

ACTIVITY 23   F1, F3

Using the timetable in Figure 8 as a rough guide, sketch out how you would approach scheduling and carrying out a programme for communicating a TQM initiative in your organization.

The following activity helps you to consolidate your learning in this section.

ACTIVITY 24

1   Describe the type of organizational culture that is most supportive of Total Quality Management.

2   What would be the consequences if a Total Quality programme were introduced into an organization with a different type of culture?

3   Which of Harrison's four types of organizational culture do you think is the least favourable to TQM, and why?

4   Who should initiate and drive the cultural changes needed as part of a TQM programme?

5   Describe the main features and benefits of empowerment.

6   What are the advantages of an employee morale survey and how should one be conducted?

7   Give four reasons why people fear change in the workplace.

8   How can an organization introducing TQM defuse employee resistance? Name
    four measures.

9   Name five requirements for a successful communication strategy.

FEEDBACK

If you had difficulties with any question in the previous activity, refresh your memory by re-reading the relevant section. Or you might find it useful to discuss the issue with a colleague.

Summary

- An organizational culture that supports Total Quality Management is a crucial precondition for a successful quality initiative. Without the right culture, all other efforts to launch a quality initiative are likely to fail. For this reason, analysing and, where necessary, modifying the organizational environment must become a key element in the process of planning and implementing any TQM programme.
- The ideal organizational culture is one which is well-integrated with the organization's mission and grounded in guiding principles such as fairness, responsibility and respect. A free flow of communications and a participative, empowering management style tend to promote good employee relations and release the potential and creativity of organization members at all levels.
- This ideal may be rare, but organizations need deliberately to work toward it in order to gain commitment throughout the organization to the quality initiative. As with any change programme, the impetus and driving force must come from senior executives and cascade through all management levels till it reaches front-line employees. Executives and managers must 'walk their talk' by implementing structures, systems and procedures that ensure that necessary cultural changes 'bed down' in the organization.

■ An organization's strategy for communicating the TQM programme should be integrated with, and facilitate, the consultation, training and implementation processes of the initiative. Enough time should be allowed for informing, persuading and gaining commitment from members of the organization. The organization should recognize and deal positively with the stress which change programmes can precipitate, and should encourage a dialogue between the change agents and other employees. True communication is a two-way activity, involving both listening and giving information and guidance.

■ The publicity campaign should use a variety of media and give regular updates on the progress of the quality programme. Finally, it should publicize and celebrate the successes achieved as a result of the Total Quality programme, and seek to improve morale and foster a sense of pride and unity.

Notes

1 *Organisational Change, Techniques and Application,* Marguiles, N. (1973).
2 *Managing the Resource Allocation Process,* Bower, J.L. (1972).
3 *The Improvement Process,* Harrington (1987), p. 59.
4 Adapted from *The Improvement Process,* Harrington (1987), pp. 27–9.

Section 4 The implementation toolkit: People skills

Introduction

In this section of the workbook you will examine the people management skills needed to implement Total Quality Management in your organization. These skills include the interpersonal and human resource management skills of:

- empowering employees to take responsibility for quality in their own work
- identifying and providing the training necessary to achieve this
- organizing and running quality improvement groups in workteams

Empowerment was introduced in Section 3. This section expands on that discussion, examines some practical issues and looks at some pragmatic measures you can take to empower your employees. It describes how this method of people management changes the relationship between managers and subordinates. It outlines some potential hazards and gives guidance on how to avoid them.

Empowerment depends on a well-trained workforce. Implementing TQM requires identifying the training needs of every part of the organization, and providing the required training and development. This section examines the issues of identifying the correct training, deciding who should provide it, and ensuring that both stages of training – understanding and application – are achieved.

One essential element of employee involvement in TQM is the effective use of quality improvement groups (also known as quality circles) at operational level. In this section you will look at how to set up such groups, what they should try to achieve, and how they can be helped to do so.

WHERE THIS SECTION FITS

People management skills are one strand of the two-pronged approach needed to implement a successful TQM initiative. Total Quality Management depends on everyone in the organization pulling together. If employees are not properly motivated, this simply will not happen. The challenge for managers is twofold: to learn and practise effective people management skills, and to implement appropriate systems and procedures, in order to enable their subordinates to achieve excellence and continual improvement. This section should give you a good grounding in the issues and practicalities of the 'soft' skills necessary to become a Total Quality organization.

Quality is everyone's responsibility

As you saw in Section 1, one of the major principles of Total Quality Management is that process chains extend beyond the functional departments and divisions of traditional organizational structures. To improve processes, an organization must pay careful attention to the hand-over points where work moves from one work group or department to another (or, as you now understand, from an internal supplier to an internal customer).

Quality is incremental. Many small improvements can result in large-scale quality increases and the substantial bottom-line gains which accompany them. The steady flow of incremental improvements will dry up, however, without the active participation of each member of the organization. Everyone must be involved in the push for quality, or potential improvements will fall through the cracks. Everyone must feel responsible to their internal as well as their external customers, or internal waste will multiply and the organization will be unable to provide affordable quality to the final customer.

The organization must promote a common view of quality which all employees understand and share. (This is why both training and publicity campaigns are so important to quality initiatives.) The organization must also make the necessary structural and procedural changes so that:

■ communication can flow upwards from the workforce to management
■ employees have the authority to make decisions concerning quality in their own work

Only if this happens can incremental improvements become established and start to build up quality and pare down poor-quality costs.

ACTIVITY 25

Are there areas in you organization where quality suffers because employees are not allowed to take responsibility for their work?

As a senior manager, do you feel you are sufficiently in touch with the front-line aspects of your organization to give an accurate answer to this question?

If not, who do you feel could answer it?

As Peter Drucker has said, 'The individual worker knows better than anyone else what makes him or her effective. The only true expert is the person who does the job.' TQM programmes seek to change management practices so that the organization can tap into – and benefit from – this pool of expertise. The necessary changes that promote this include:

- measuring processes, not people (for example, Deming advocates eliminating numerical targets for employees)
- removing barriers to communication, including management's tendency to talk but not listen
- recognizing that employees want to do a good job
- instituting measures that promote employee empowerment

Empowerment

Empowerment is a management method which involves employees participating in or controlling aspects of work that were traditionally the preserve of management. Empowerment means sharing responsibility, information, and a higher level of decision-making with subordinates, but it does not mean weak management. Certain decisions, such as strategic or policy decisions, will still need to be made by executives and managers. Empowerment, however, entails a greater degree of transparency and communication in the decision-making process. Management and employees share information, and managers tend to consult with employees before making a decision, and to explain their decisions to them afterwards. In this sense, empowerment requires participatory leadership.

Routine decisions regarding both work and the operation of their own working groups are handed over to employees. For example, employees monitor their own work (rather than leaving this to supervisors), and have the authority to stop production lines if they spot a quality problem. Self-managed teams plan their own work rotas, overtime and leave provision. In some organizations, workteams are given discretion over recruitment of team members and routine budget expenditures. In certain companies, employees have a say in their organization's reward system; for example, at Proctor and Gamble in the USA, employees' pay progression is decided by their peers, not their superiors.

Empowerment requires changes in work patterns and habits. Employees are treated less like automatons carrying out the instructions of their superiors, and more as responsible adults who are entitled to information and are able to make valuable contributions to their work. For example, in empowered organizations, the working day (or week) often begins with a briefing by the supervisor or team leader, or with a hand-over meeting between the outgoing and incoming shifts. This level of communication also extends to the sharing of business information; in some organizations, management shares financial and marketing information with employees, who are trained to understand and apply it to their own work areas.

Empowered organizations tend to have flatter management structures and to emphasize teamwork. The roles of supervisors and front-line managers shift from that of inspector to that of team facilitator. Teams are taught the techniques of problem solving and effective group working, and are expected to use them and to take responsibility for achieving and maintaining quality. Procedures become more flexible and less rule-bound as front-line staff are given more discretion. In empowered organizations, employees 'own' both the successes and the problems arising from their work.

Increasing employees' levels of responsibility will not be effective, however, if they are afraid of being punished for mistakes. Empowerment must take place in tandem with cultural changes which remove any traces of a 'blame culture'. As you will see in Section 5, effective process analysis depends on employees' truthful assessment of work practices and systems. It is not possible to achieve this if employees are tempted to falsify or withhold information for fear of reprisals or penalties.

What aspects of empowerment do you think would be suitable for your organization?

What procedural changes would need to be instituted in order to facilitate them?

There are many advantages to empowerment. It tends to make organizations more flexible and responsive to changes demanded by the external environment. Empowered organizations are certainly more responsive to the customer, as customer complaints can be handled faster, without front-line staff needing to refer decisions to superiors. Employees' self-esteem, motivation and morale increase. Effective and satisfying teamwork result in higher-quality output, as group pressure and cohesiveness promote higher standards than traditional supervision could. Employees' ideas are tapped and fed back into the organization; for example, employees close to the customers can identify gaps in product lines.

The move to empowerment does carry certain risks, however. Empowerment promotes a new relationship between managers and subordinates. Front-line and middle managers are often threatened by a perceived erosion of their role, and, at worst, a fear of redundancy. This tier of management are often the group who must change their long-established working practices most radically. A number of quality initiatives have foundered because this level of management have decided to drag their feet or 'wait out' the empowerment fad. For this reason, any empowerment initiative needs:

- a powerful executive champion
- a deliberate programme of informing, persuading and supporting middle and front-line managers

To ensure that empowerment succeeds, the organization must emphasize and maximize the advantages it holds for this level of employees. Managers must be empowered too. Executives and senior managers must hand over tasks and resources to their management subordinates in the same way that middle managers do to theirs. And they must provide the management development necessary to enable middle managers to perform effectively.

The advantages of empowerment for middle managers must be stressed (and the organization must take measures to ensure that they are indeed realized). Empowerment leads to better time management. Managers have more time for higher-level activities and are less likely to become over-worked and stressed. This will improve the quality of their management performance, as well as the quality of their working and private lives.

Some middle managers will thrive on becoming the team leaders and facilitators needed by an empowered workforce. Some will be less comfortable with this role, but will be able to learn it. Managers at this level should be given adequate training and support, and the opportunity – in a safe, blame-free environment – to discuss issues raised for them by this process of role transition.

ACTIVITY 27

What issues do you think the shift to empowerment would raise with middle and front-line managers in your organization?

There may be some employees at all levels who do not want to become empowered, and who would prefer their jobs to continue as they were. It is possible that niches in the organization can be found for employees with this attitude, or they may prefer to leave and join a more traditional organization. If such employees do remain, they should not be allowed to disrupt either the process of empowerment or the new work practices that arise from it. This may entail moving them to different parts of the organization.

Training

Neither quality improvements nor empowerment will work without trained employees. The purpose of training in a TQM organization is not to teach employees to do their jobs in a better way, but rather to give them the tools and skills so that they can discover better ways of doing their jobs themselves. After all, they are the experts. The desired sequence of events entails:

- employees receiving training
- employees identifying problems in their own work area and suggesting solutions (sometimes in collaboration with experts, internal or external customers, or internal or external suppliers)
- employees trying out solutions
- workable solutions being established as standard practice
- employees continually refining and extending the improvements in their work area

Training can sometimes appear expensive to organizations that have not invested in it before. Successful Total Quality organizations, however, find that it yields a significant return on investment. Motorola, for example, a progressive organization spending $100 million on training annually, calculates that every $1 invested in training brings a return of $33.[1]

Not every organization has the size or purchasing power of a Motorola, however. Organizations of every size need to ensure that they receive good value for their training expenditure. This can be bewildering given the range of training options on offer. A few guidelines should make the job easier.

Training must be fully integrated with the Total Quality strategy. Clear outcomes for the training must be identified by the internal planning team, advised by the management consultants facilitating the quality initiative. These outcomes must include proficiency in both the technical, 'hard' skills used in process analysis and the interpersonal, 'soft' skills needed to communicate and work effectively with other people. Often 'problem-solving skills' are thought of as analytical methods, such as flow charting, which are related to the technical aspects of a job. It should be remembered, however, that many common on-the-job problems are related to interpersonal difficulties, so that problem-solving skills in this dimension should not be neglected. One American survey of training in TQM initiatives concluded that training in technical or statistical approaches was ineffective if organizations did not have a good foundation of well-developed 'people skills' which meant that employees could work well together.[2]

The training method recommended by H. J. Harrington and others makes use of the 'waterfall effect'. Training in both technical and interpersonal skills begins at the top of the organization. When top management have learned and begun to use the new skills, the middle layers of management are trained, and so on down the hierarchy. It is vital that every manager thoroughly understands and can use the new skills, even the most technical ones.

Finding training provision

Your management consultants may be able to provide training, or you might need, with their advice, to engage specialist training providers.

ACTIVITY 28

What are some of the criteria you would look for in selecting external trainers to provide training for your quality initiative? Identify at least four criteria.

1

2

3

4

FEEDBACK

You may well have identified certain criteria similar to the ones you would consider in selecting a management consultant:

■ demonstrable specialist expertise and experience in providing training in the particular areas you need
■ experience in working successfully with organizations similar to your own
■ evidence of a reputable, well-run company or organization

In addition you might look for:

■ presentable and competent trainers who communicate well with the people in your organization
■ effective teaching materials, if part of their approach depends on using these
■ affiliation or accreditation with academic institutions or NVQ assessment centres, Training and Enterprise Councils, industry lead bodies or the British Quality Foundation

Many reputable training companies will allow you to attend a sample session in order to assess their abilities and approach before you commit yourself.

Front-line managers and supervisors are given special training and support, because they have responsibility for training the workteams they supervise. Effective training is composed of two elements:

- understanding new ideas and skills
- applying these in the workplace

'Many times, quality implementation stalls because the transfer of quality theory to practice never takes place', observed Dr J. H. Zenger, who conducted a training audit of American quality programmes.[3] Organizations must ensure that their investment in training is carried right through into front-line operations, and that improvements are established as standard working practice. This will be impossible without the active co-operation of employees, so supervisors must consult and listen carefully to employees' views on the feasibility of changing working practices.

Using supervisors to train front-line employees helps to ensure that the emphasis of the training is on applying the new skills and understanding to the job in a practical way. It also reinforces their role as team leaders and facilitators. It may be more feasible for supervisors to train their teams in technical skills than in the full range of interpersonal skills needed. If this is the case, the supervisors should be included in any 'soft' skill training or development programmes offered to the workteam by external (or in-house) training consultants.

To motivate employees to make the most of training, some organizations set up awards schemes designed to publicize and reward participation in training. The Oxford-based bus company, Thames Transit, for example, has established a badge system which allows drivers to display the level of training they have achieved. Posters in buses explain the badge system to passengers, allowing them to identify their bus driver's level of training.

Training is a process like any other. It must be measured and evaluated against established goals in order to ensure that the organization is getting value for money and the training it needs to progress the TQM programme.

ACTIVITY 29

Fill in the following training analysis form for each section of the workforce in your organization.

Training analysis form

1   What training outcomes are we seeking?

2   How do these outcomes relate to our overall goals for the TQM programme?

3   What type(s) of training will deliver these outcomes?

4   Who will deliver this training?

5   How will we know whether this training has been effective?

Quality improvement groups

The training and empowerment of work groups leads naturally to the formation of quality improvement groups. At front-line level, such groups are composed of every member of a workteam, led by their supervisor. These groups meet regularly once a week for an hour or so (in company time) in order to discuss quality-related issues.

When quality improvement groups are being set up, senior and middle managers should be aware of how much training and support they are likely to need. Most employees do not know how to work in teams, and will need training in:

- running meetings
- resolving conflict
- presenting findings to management

as well as in the technical skills required for Total Quality Management (these are discussed in Section 5).

Groups will also need the support of a middle or senior manager who attends their meetings regularly. Records of meetings should be kept, so that managers get to know a group's strengths and weaknesses, can identify their training needs, and use their abilities most effectively. Managers must understand that front-line quality improvement groups can only solve problems related to their own work areas.

In the early stages, groups tend to focus on understanding the technical elements of their training, and on applying them to their work. In order not to get discouraged or overwhelmed by the process, groups should start by concentrating on a limited number of manageable issues. As they become more experienced in using their new skills, they will start to focus on identifying and generating solutions for work-related problems. The groups should become a regular feature of every team's working week and in time will begin to contribute a steady flow of improvements to their part of the organization. Toyota, for example, estimates that its employees contribute one million ideas a year to the company.

Naturally, not every idea generated will be a world-class winner. Experts estimate that, on average, only one out of every sixty ideas is a good one. This means that the quality improvement groups must be encouraged to generate as many ideas as possible, and taught to screen them to capture the good ones.

In an empowered workforce, some improvements can be implemented by the workteam without reference to managers. The organization should ensure, however, that departmental managers monitor changes made by workteams. There are two reasons for this. The first one is to ensure that there are no adverse knock-on effects to other parts of the organization. The second is so that effective improvements can be shared with other teams and departments on the one hand, and, on the other, that ideas which don't work need not be tried and rejected by more than one workteam. The efficient sharing of know-how is one factor which differentiates a successful Total Quality programme from an unsuccessful one.

ACTIVITY 30

Note down some ways in which the ideas and experiences of quality improvement groups could be shared on a regular basis in your organization.

FEEDBACK

There are a number of ways know-how can be shared on a regular basis, including:

- presentations between quality improvement groups
- bulletin boards
- a special quality-group newsletter, or regular column in the company newspaper
- monthly updates in each quality group of what other groups are discussing and how their ideas might be applied in other areas
- formal or informal liaison between representatives from each group

The best methods are those which are not too time-consuming or administratively demanding but which still provide a thorough dissemination of new ideas and improvements.

In addition to these methods, the organization may need to appoint a senior manager to oversee the sharing and implementation of know-how.

There is likely to be a category of suggested improvements which are sufficiently large-scale, expensive or complicated, to need to be referred upward to management. (An example of such a decision would be one which involved retooling a production line.) The organization must ensure that there is an effective pathway through which the contributions of quality groups are passed on to management. In general this will involve close communication between a designated representative of the group (possibly but not necessarily the supervisor) and the next level of management.

Groups will soon become discouraged and sceptical if management does not respond quickly to their ideas. Middle managers must not sit on ideas, but pass them up to more senior levels, if necessary. Managers at all levels must consider employees' suggestions carefully, consult with the appropriate people, take decisions and give prompt and thorough feedback, explaining their decision. Managers should also be sure to praise and celebrate workteams' winning ideas.

Not every idea generated by a quality improvement group must be accepted. To be implemented, ideas must be feasible in operational, financial and staffing terms, and must give a good indication that they will bring measurable improvement.

Quality improvement groups form the grass-roots level foundation of any Total Quality initiative. Because their members are all from the same workteam, however, they can sometimes lack the wider perspective that contributes to process-wide improvements. For this reason, two other types of quality groups are necessary in many TQM initiatives:

- key process groups
- innovation groups

KEY PROCESS GROUPS

In the initial stages of a TQM initiative (such as the pilot phase), key process groups should be formed to analyse and suggest improvements to one or more of the major processes in the organization. These temporary, cross-functional groups are made up of the managers of every department involved in the process, along with representative employees familiar with the various aspects of the process. Their brief is to measure and analyse each stage of the process, and identify areas where improvements can be made. Once the group has made its recommendations, it is disbanded. A manager is then appointed to oversee the implementation of the improvements.

INNOVATION GROUPS

Innovation groups are voluntary groups of employees from various departments and levels in the organization. Their purpose is to find innovative and better ways of doing things. Such groups usually need to be led by facilitators specially trained in creativity and innovation techniques. As these groups are voluntary, they might meet outside regular working hours. Some organizations offer an incentive scheme, where successful innovations are rewarded by special bonuses.

The following activity helps you to consolidate your learning in this section.

ACTIVITY 31

1 Why are people management skills important to a Total Quality Management programme?

2 What is empowerment?

3 Outline the advantages and risks of empowerment.

4 What sector of the organization is most likely to resist the move to empowerment, and what measures can be taken to minimize or eliminate this resistance?

5 What is the major purpose of training in a Total Quality organization?

6 What is the 'waterfall effect' with regard to training, and why is it recommended?

7 Outline the relationship between training in technical skills and training in interpersonal skills in a TQM initiative.

8 Describe the role of supervisors in training and leading quality improvement groups.

9 List three or four ways in which improvements or know-how can be shared among quality improvement groups.

10 What steps can managers take to ensure that quality improvement groups are effective?

If you had difficulties with any question in the previous activity, refresh your memory by re-reading the relevant section. Or you might find it useful to discuss the issue with a colleague.

Summary

- 'Soft' people management skills are vital to the success of a TQM programme. Effective people management motivates and enables employees to accept responsibility for the quality of their own work, to identify and solve problems, and to suggest improvements. The three major aspects of good people management in a TQM initiative are empowerment of the workforce, training, and the use of quality improvement groups.

- Empowerment is a management method which gives as much responsibility and discretion to employees as possible. Routine job-related decisions are left in the hands of workteams, who also control the planning and scheduling of their own work. They may also participate in other administrative or staffing decisions and activities related to their own work-team. In empowered organizations, management shares information with employees, and ensures that they receive the training to interpret and use it in their work. The benefits of empowerment include greater flexibility, quality improvements, and higher morale and productivity . True empowerment is impossible unless an organization:
  - ensures that employees will not be punished or ridiculed for mistakes
  - empowers middle managers and supervisors as well as front-line workers
  - trains employees effectively

- In Total Quality organizations, training works with empowerment to enable employees to identify problems and discover and implement solutions. Employees are trained both in the technical skills of process analysis and problem solving on the one hand, and, on the other, in the interpersonal skills that enable them to communicate and work well with colleagues. The purpose of training is to help employees release and apply the job-related expertise that only they possess. When this potential is unlocked, steady, incremental gains in quality should result.

- The procedure through which empowerment and training are applied in the workplace is the quality improvement group. Workteams, trained and led by their supervisors, meet regularly to discuss the application of their new problem-solving skills to their work, and to identify improvements. Such group meetings become a regular part of the weekly work schedule.

- Empowered workteams can implement many small-scale improvements without seeking the 'permission' of managers. Departmental managers, however, should monitor the improvements in order to:
  - ensure that they are not causing problems for other parts of the organization
  - measure their effectiveness
  - make sure that they are shared and applied as widely as possible
- To reap the benefits of quality improvement groups, an organization must ensure that there is sufficient sharing of information both vertically and horizontally. Vertical communication is necessary to make sure that management responds quickly to quality groups' suggestions. Horizontal communication ensures that learning and successful innovations are applied as widely as possible through the organization.
- The techniques of quality improvement groups can also be used in key process groups (in the early stages of quality initiatives) and in innovation groups (when the initiative is well-established).

Notes

1 *Winning at Change*, by Blair and Meadows, Institute of Management/Pitman Publishing (1996), p. 94.

2 *Fortune* (1989), p. 9.

3 *Fortune* (1989), p. 9.

Section 5 The implementation toolkit: Technical skills

Introduction

In this section of the workbook you will look in closer detail at the technical skills which are used to identify and implement quality improvements. The first part of the section discusses the need for measurement and process management as a key aspect of Total Quality Management. It examines the use of measurement and analysis tools, describes some commonly used methods and identifies the types of processes they are most suited for

The section then considers the issues of identifying, analysing and solving problems and opportunities for improvement. It discusses various techniques which quality improvement groups can use to identify, analyse and solve problems, such as brainstorming, flow charting, Pareto analysis, fishbone diagrams, and others.

Finally, the section describes the two strands of problem solving in a Total Quality organization. These are:

- corrective action, the practice of putting right the underlying causes of problems
- continuous improvement, the practice of embedding process improvement techniques in operational activities so that a spiral of increasing quality is achieved

WHERE THIS SECTION FITS

Technical skills for process analysis and management form the second vital component in the implementation of a Total Quality Management initiative. Everyone in the organization, from top managers to front-line staff, are trained to use these skills, which range from the use of complex statistical techniques to flow charting and cause-and-effect analysis. Once processes have been analysed, and problems or opportunities for improvement have been identified, a number of techniques may be used to identify solutions and evaluate their merit.

Once improvements have been identified, they must be tried and tested to determine their effectiveness. This often leads to further corrections and refinements, resulting in even greater improvements. This process of analysing problems, then identifying and testing solutions, forms the corrective action loop which should lead to continuous improvement and quality gains.

The use of these technical skills forms an important part of the activities of quality improvement groups, key process groups and innovation groups.

Measurement and process analysis

As you saw in Section 1, a key element of Total Quality Management involves viewing organizational activities as processes involving inputs, activities and outputs. In most organizations, processes tend to evolve over the life cycles of products or services, as well as during the growth and development of the organization itself. Usually they make more sense in historical terms than in terms of efficiency. Incremental modifications and adaptations build up and eventually cause most processes to go out of kilter. Process management is a way of analysing and readjusting processes so that efficiency and quality are maximized.

The first step in process management is identifying the organization's key processes. Once these have been identified, they can be analysed and measured to determine how well they are currently operating. Analysis and measurement work together to build up a clear picture of what is actually happening with current processes. This is the first step in identifying ways of increasing their effectiveness and efficiency.

PROCESS ANALYSIS

Before a process is measured, it must be understood. Process analysis begins with the use of a simple process diagram which identifies a process's key features. The process diagrams in Figures 9 and 10 illustrate how an understanding of a process can be built up by identifying its key elements.

Once the key elements such as suppliers, inputs, scope, outputs, requirements, and clients have been identified, the activities of the process can be examined. Flow charting can be used to identify the individual tasks into which a process is broken down, the sequence of these tasks, hand-over points, delays and so on. Flow charting is already a familiar tool to many managers, designers and engineers. If you are unfamiliar with this technique, you can find out more about it in *Managing Quality* by Bell, McBridge and Wilson (see Recommended Reading) and in Workbook 3 of this series, *Understanding Business Process Management.*

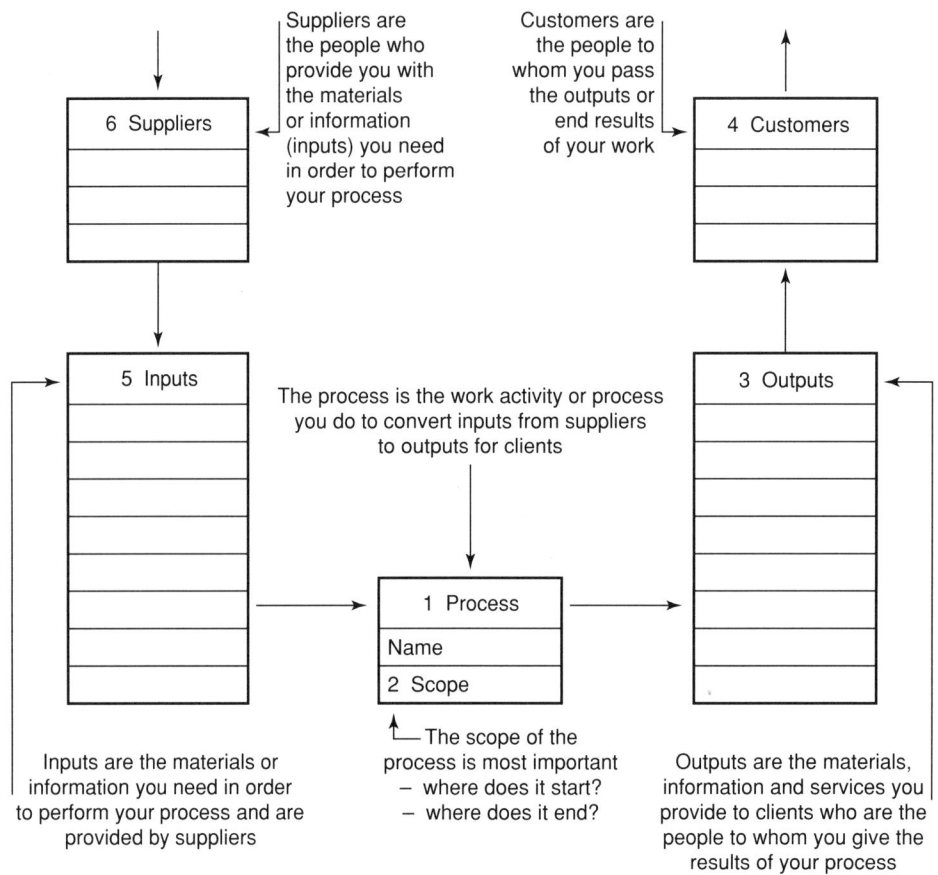

Figure 9   The elements of a simple process diagram

7 Input requirements	6 Supplier	5 Inputs	1 Process Typing a letter	2 Outputs	3 Customers	4 Output requirements
By 1500 hours	Manager	Draft		Typed letter	Manager	By 1530 hours
Addressee details	Office Supplies	Headed paper		Copies	Copy addressees	3 copies
Copy addressee		Copy paper		Draft		Error free
Legible						Standard layout
Standard copy paper						Courier typeface
Draft error free			Scope			Confidential
			Initial task: Draft letter			
			Final task: Typed letter			

Process requirements		
Equipment	Process / procedures	Employee skills
Typewriter	Layout models	Typing skills
Desk	Paper type models	Knowledge of procedures
Chair		
Electricity on		

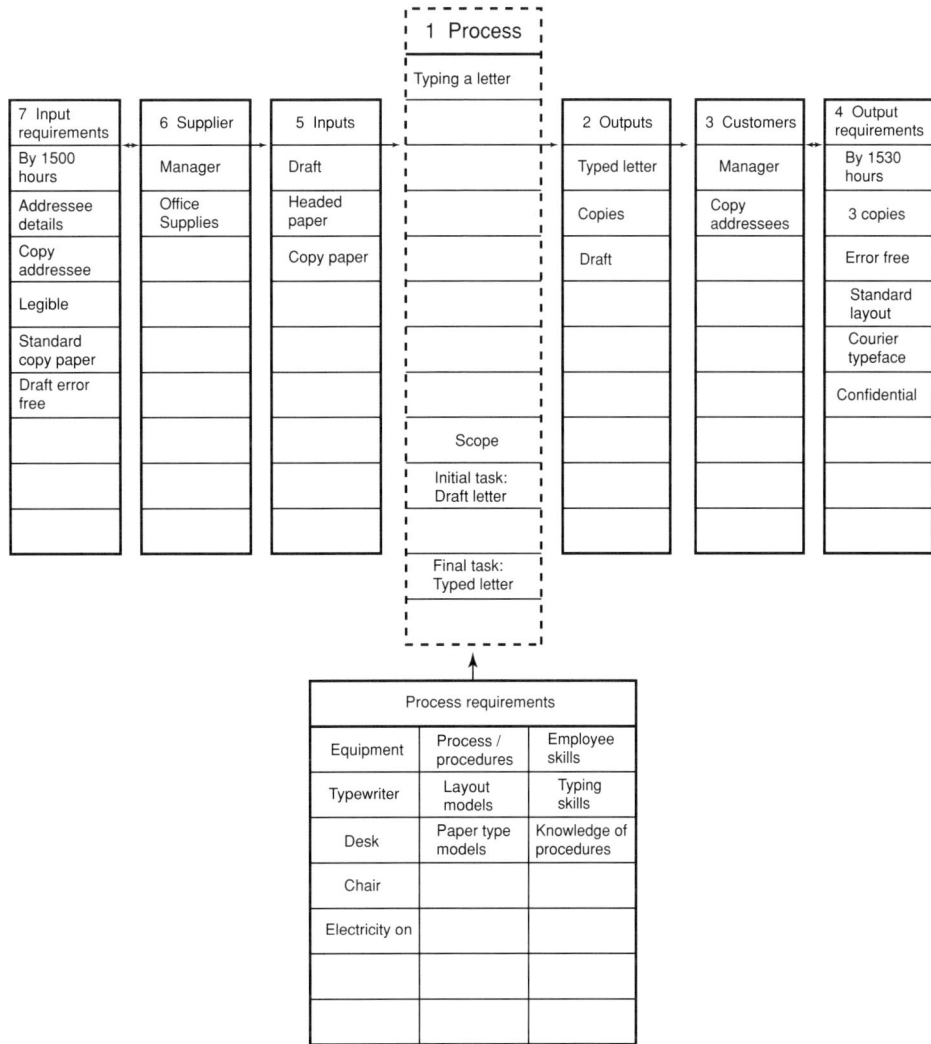

Figure 10 The elements of a process diagram showing input, output and process requirements

A simple flow chart is illustrated in Figure 11.

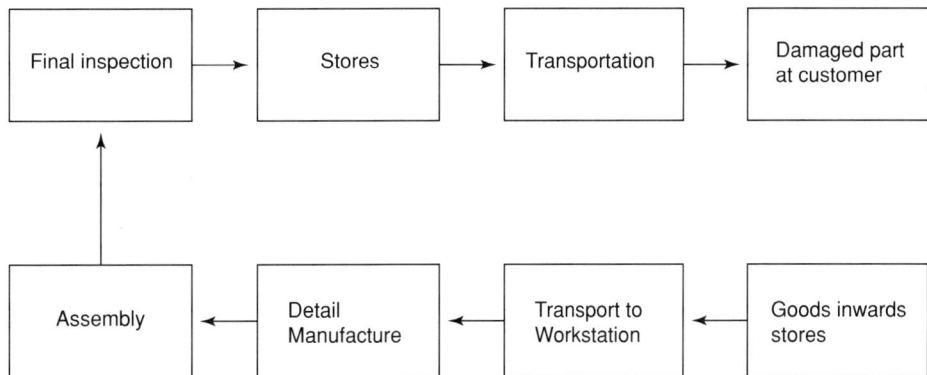

Figure 11 A simple flow chart

ACTIVITY 32   F4

Select either an element of your own job or a simple process in your
organization. Construct:

1   a process diagram identifying its key elements

2   a flow chart detailing the sequence of tasks and activities it entails

FEEDBACK

Harrington recommends that each department in the organization conduct an analysis and audit of its activities. This involves identifying the major processes or activities it carries out (no more than ten) and completing a process analysis for each one. The department then measures and establishes improvement goals for each activity, using the methods outlined in the rest of this section.

MEASUREMENT

When a process or subprocess has been broken down into its constituent parts, it can then be measured. Measurement involves devising ways of collecting meaningful, quantifiable data about the process, and then collecting that data. An appropriate level of measurement needs to quantify both productivity and quality. Productivity is concerned with how efficiently and quickly an activity is performed. Quality is concerned with how well it is performed. Improvement occurs either when both of these levels increase, or when one increases without causing any decrease in the other.

Some organizations, particularly those involved in non-manufacturing enterprises, initially find it difficult to think of ways of measuring their processes. However, this can nearly always be achieved, given the right attitude and training. The key, according to H. J. Harrington is to differentiate between activities (what you do) and outputs (what you achieve; the useful results of what you do). Outputs can be quantified and measured in virtually every process. (In recent years, for example, public services such as local authorities, hospitals and educational institutions have been much occupied with identifying appropriate Key Performance Indicators to measure their outputs.) If there are no outputs of any particular activity, this is an indication that the activity may be superfluous or a waste of resources. As Harrington concludes, 'Any job that cannot be measured is probably not worth doing and should be eliminated.'[1]

ACTIVITY 33

Return to the process you considered in Activity 32. Think of three or four ways in which the outputs of the activities you identified could be measured in terms of both productivity and quality.

FEEDBACK

This activity may have led you to realize that some measurements are more meaningful than others. For example, for a salesperson of large, expensive products such as heavy, earth-moving machinery, the number of sales made per week may be a much less meaningful measure than the number of sales made per month or even per quarter.

It is important that appropriate measures are devised which take into consideration the nature of an organization's enterprise, its market, type of customers, and so on. Managers and other employees must be involved in identifying appropriate measurements for the processes they are involved in. The finance department will need to be involved to devise appropriate financial measurements and gather and process the relevant information. Benchmarking information will also influence an organization's choice of measurement standards. Finally, the customer must not be forgotten; information about customer expectations should be central to the formulation of measurement standards.

Productivity (that is, the **number** of outputs) can be measured in terms of:

- time
- money
- efficient use of resources

Quality can be measured in terms of:

- accuracy
- numbers of variations or defects
- levels of repeated work necessary
- numbers of complaints from internal or external customers

ACTIVITY 34

Of the types of measurement you identified in Activity 33, which are the most meaningful, given the process they relate to?

PROCESS MEASUREMENT AND ANALYSIS TECHNIQUES

There are a number of measurement techniques which can be used, according to the nature of the activity being analysed. These include the following.

Error charting and logging

Keeping error logs and charts allows managers and employees to keep track of the level and nature of errors. Acceptable tolerances in output will have been identified for the activity or process, and variances from these are systematically noted. Error charts and logs can be used for both manufacturing or service activities. (In a service context, for example, customer complaints can be registered at a Customer Service Counter in a retail outlet or service-based business). Figure 12 shows an example of an error chart from a financial services organization.

Error	Month				Total
	Jan	Feb	Mar	Apr	
Clerical error	8	6	12	9	35
Slow service	22	17	18	27	84
Teller error	14	8	12	10	44
Clerical error	8	6	12	9	35
Computer error	2	0	1	3	6
Lost paperwork	5	8	3	5	21
Lack of courtesy	3	6	1	2	12
Other	1	0	2	1	4

Figure 12 Error chart of customer complaints from a building society branch

Run charts and process control charts

These charts give a running picture of the performance of an activity based on a particular data sample. They are designed to detect negative trends so that they can be corrected before they get out of control. There are a number of different types of charts, which illustrate either variable (quantitative) data or attributive (qualitative) data. The use of statistical techniques makes it easy to see when defects or variations begin to swing into unacceptable levels. These types of charts include:

- U charts, which measure the number of defects per unit
- c charts, which measure the number of defects in a sample
- P charts, which measure the percentage of defective units in a sample
- $n\bar{p}$ charts, which measure the number of defective units in a sample
- $\bar{X}$ and R charts, double charts which measure the mean value of variation in a sample (the $\bar{X}$ chart) and the range of variation distribution (the R chart)

U, c, P, and n̄p̄ charts are attributive control charts; X̄ and R charts are variable control charts.

Figures 13 and 14 show typical examples of control charts.

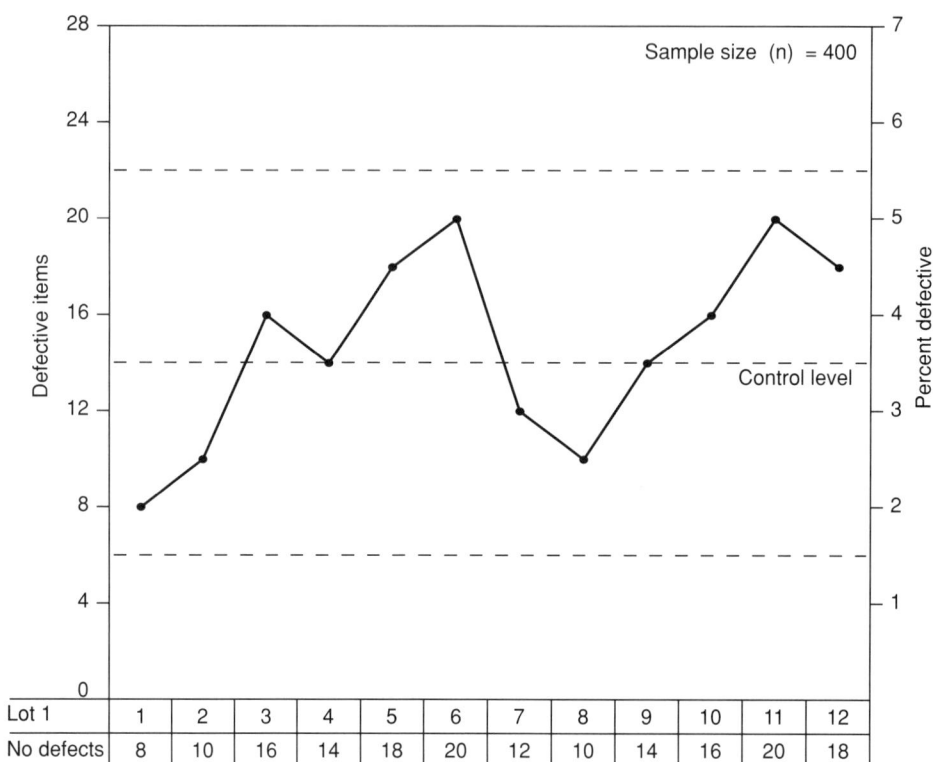

Figure 13   An example of an n̄p̄ control chart

Run charts and process control charts, as well as error charts and logs, should be maintained at the site of the activity, and ideally should form part of the activity itself.

STATISTICAL PROCESS CONTROL (SPC)

This method is designed to measure and analyse production processes in manufacturing enterprises. It is a complex technique which will need to be taught and introduced into production systems by qualified experts. In essence statistical process control monitors and analyses a process through four phases:

■ the out-of-control phase, when the process shows unacceptable levels of variation from standards

■ the stable phase, when the statistical variation in the process is stabilized, but the output is still of an unacceptable quality to meet customer requirements

- step-by-step improvement, when improvements are introduced one by one and monitored to determine their effect on the whole process; during this phase, real quality gains are achieved
- delivery to customer, when the output has achieved the quality expected by the customer; this phase is also called continuous improvement, because it is necessary continually to monitor output against changing customer expectations and requirements

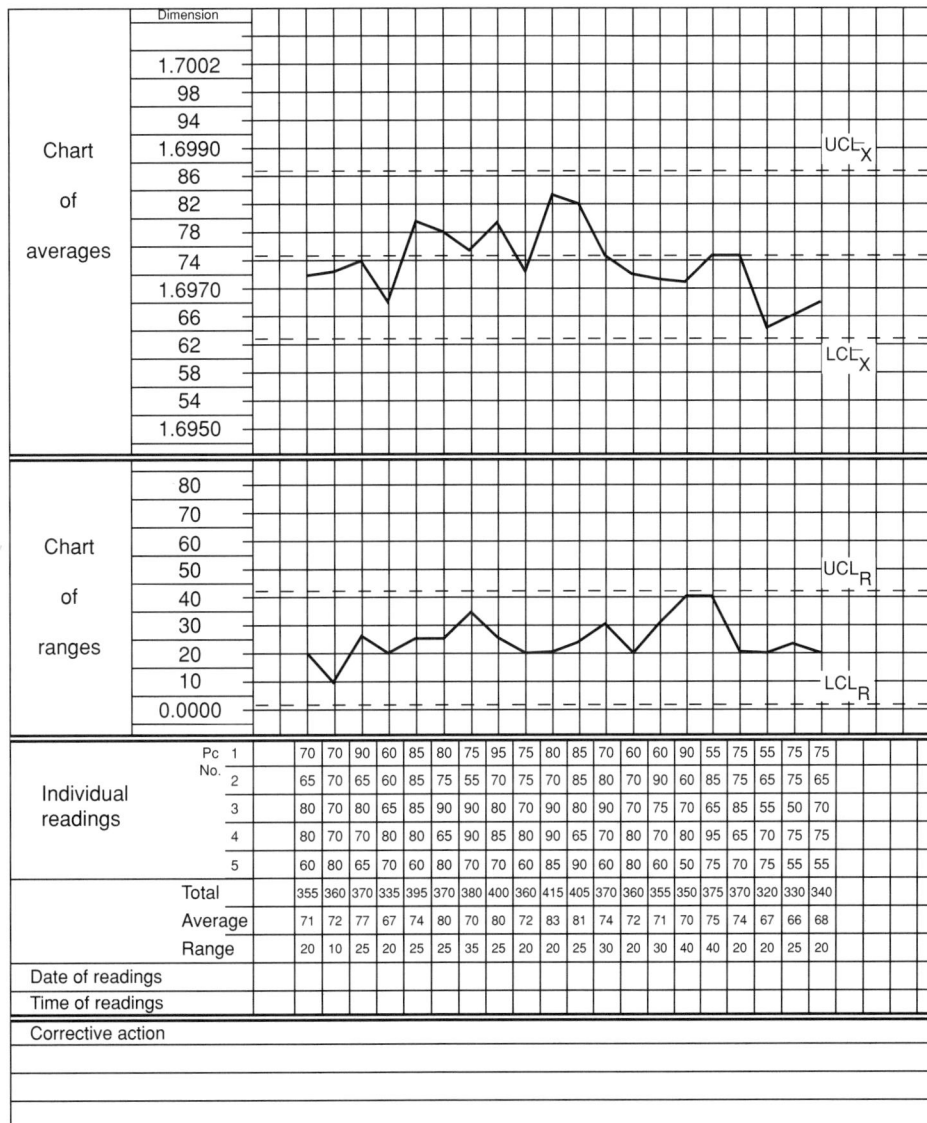

	Pc No.																				
Individual readings	1	70	70	90	60	85	80	75	95	75	80	85	70	60	60	90	55	75	55	75	75
	2	65	70	65	60	85	75	55	70	75	70	85	80	70	90	60	85	75	65	75	65
	3	80	70	80	65	85	90	90	80	70	90	80	90	70	75	70	65	85	55	50	70
	4	80	70	70	80	80	65	90	85	80	90	65	70	80	70	80	95	65	70	75	75
	5	60	80	65	70	60	80	70	70	60	85	90	60	80	60	50	75	70	75	55	55
Total		355	360	370	335	395	370	380	400	360	415	405	370	360	355	350	375	370	320	330	340
Average		71	72	77	67	74	80	70	80	72	83	81	74	72	71	70	75	74	67	66	68
Range		20	10	25	20	25	25	35	25	20	20	25	30	20	30	40	40	20	20	25	20

Date of readings
Time of readings
Corrective action

Figure 14　An example of an $\bar{X}$ and R control chart

More information about these process measurement techniques may be found in *The Improvement Process* by Harrington, in *Tools and Methods for the Improvement of Quality* by Gitlow and Oppenheim, and in *Managing Quality* by Bell et al., all listed in the Recommended Reading list.

Whatever measurement techniques are selected, it is vital that the

information they yield is acted on to identify and achieve quality improvements. If charts become mere 'wallpaper', or the process of measurement deteriorates into a bureaucratic time-wasting exercise, the Total Quality initiative has failed.

Furthermore, as measurements should ideally be taken at the site of the process activity, accuracy depends on the honesty, co-operation and training of the people working the processes and taking the measurements. This is why effective training, on the one hand, and a no-blame culture, on the other, are such important elements in a successful TQM initiative. In short, it should be emphasized that the process analysis activities are designed to measure processes, not people. To further safeguard the accuracy of the measurements, process analysis systems should include an independent audit system that will ensure that measurement recording activities comply with the correct procedures.

ACTIVITY 35

Who are the most appropriate employees to take the process measurements you identified in Activity 34?

Identifying and analysing problems

Understanding and measuring processes is the first step on the path to improved quality. But this needs to be followed up with systematic activities that allow quality improvement groups to find and analyse problems and identify opportunities for improvement. There are several techniques that can be used by quality groups for this purpose.

Identifying, analysing and solving problems are related activities; often understanding a problem clearly is enough to begin to discover a solution. In more difficult cases, possible solutions can be generated and evaluated using the same analysis methods.

TECHNIQUES FOR IDENTIFYING AND ANALYSING PROBLEMS

Brainstorming

Brainstorming is a well-known method for generating a large number of ideas in a short time. It can be used both to identify problems and to find solutions for them. Brainstorming can be done by individuals, but it is far more successful when used in a group, so it is an ideal activity for quality improvement groups.

The principles of brainstorming are simple. The technique works best when conducted with six to ten participants. The group focuses on an issue which might be broad and amorphous, such as 'What is the future of information technology in the twenty-first century?' or narrow and specific, such as 'How could we improve our productivity in welding door flanges?' Members of the group then contribute suggestions or ideas.

The most important rule of brainstorming is that participants do not censor themselves or others. All ideas, however far-fetched or apparently silly, are recorded, without discussion or criticism. For this reason it is important to maintain a blame-free environment where participants are not reluctant to venture their suggestions. The best brainstorming sessions have the character of an exciting, enjoyable, fast-paced game. A facilitator is needed to enforce the few rules, maintain momentum, keep the group on track, and record their ideas. Sometimes sessions are video-taped so that body language or otherwise inaudible contributions can be captured and analysed.

Only after the flow of ideas has completely finished are ideas discussed and screened for merit and applicability. Idea-screening and analytical techniques are used to 'edit' the list and identify the contributions with the most potential. Often the juxtaposition of apparently unrelated ideas is the spark that results in a valuable improvement.

Flow charting

As well as being used to gain an initial understanding of processes, flow charting can be used to analyse problems. It is a useful exercise when a series of events – for example, the multiple stages in a process – gives rise to a problem (such as a delay), and it is unclear which step caused it.

Flow charting appears to be a straightforward activity, but it can be surprisingly rewarding. There are (perhaps apocryphal) stories of managing directors riding on pallets to track the route of an order of goods so as to identify bottlenecks in their factories. Tracing the sequence of steps in a process can identify inefficient or repetitive process loops. Noting the length of time each step takes can also highlight chronic delays in the process. At the very least, flow charting allows a systematic examination of all stages, in order to isolate the point where a problem occurs. The flow charting of sub-processes, or other analytical techniques, can then be used to identify the cause of the problem. Flow charting is equally useful for analysing manufacturing and non-manufacturing processes.

Critical examination matrix

Another analysis tool which is well suited to both service and manufacturing operations is the critical examination matrix. This is a simple method of questioning every aspect of a process using the questions 'who?', 'what?', 'when?', 'where?', 'how?', and subjecting the answers to all these questions to the question 'why?' This allows the team to identify alternatives and select the best method for doing something from a widened range of choices. The format for a critical examination matrix is shown in Figure 15.

Current approach	Questions	Alternatives	Optimal choice
What are we doing?	Why is it necessary?	What else could be done?	What should be done?
How is it done?	Why that way?	How else could it be done?	How should it be done?
When is it done?	Why then?	When else could it be done?	When should it be done?
Where is it done?	Why there?	Where else could it be done?	Where should it be done?
Who does it?	Why them?	Who else could do it?	Who should do it?

Figure 15   A critical examination matrix

Histograms and pie charts

Histograms are bar charts. They present numerical information in graphic form in order to highlight significant trends and patterns of distribution. Histograms divide raw data (for example, numbers of staff turnover) into equal intervals (for example, months). This information is drawn as columns along an axis, so trends can be discovered by noting the placement of the highest and lowest columns. It is possible to present extremely complicated information, such the range and distribution of variations in manufactured components, in histograms. Managers can use this visual information for a number of purposes, including to diagnose problems, forecast upcoming trends and identify areas where improvement is necessary. Figure 16 illustrates a simple bar chart.

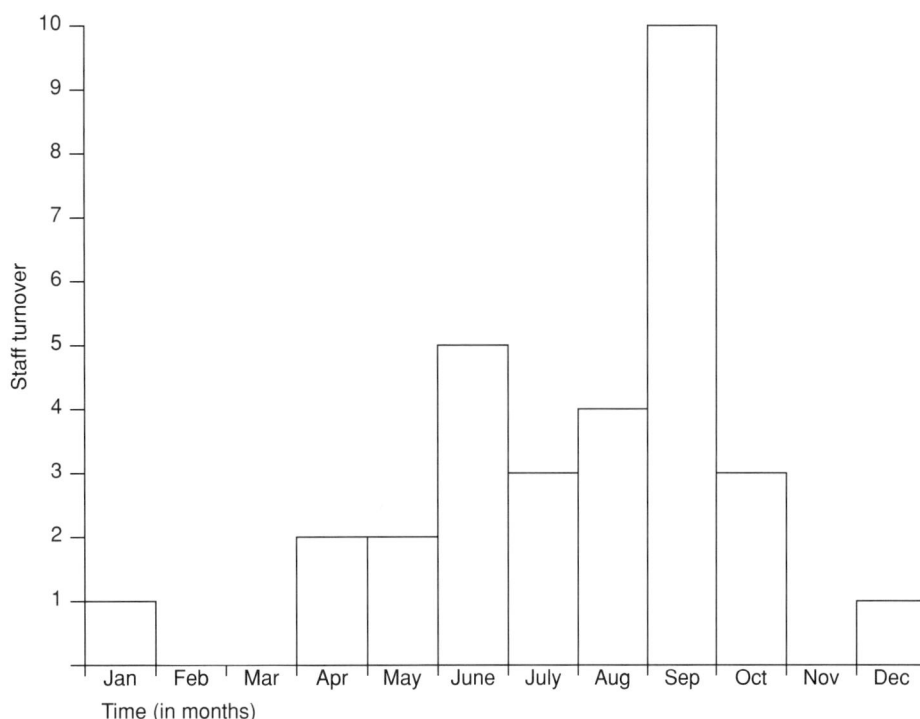

Figure 16   A bar chart showing the rate and distribution of staff turnover at a restaurant

Sometimes it is more useful to present categories of data as proportions of a whole (for example, percentage of total annual sales). Pie charts make such information easy to understand at a glance. There are a number of computer software programs for constructing pie charts from raw data, so managers are spared the onerous task of drawing an accurate chart by hand. Figure 17 shows a simple pie chart.

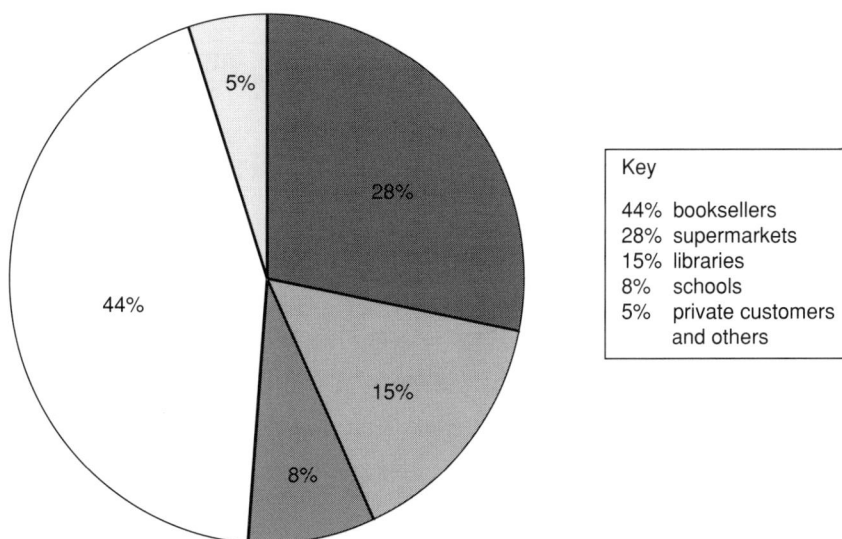

Key

44% booksellers
28% supermarkets
15% libraries
8%   schools
5%   private customers
       and others

Figure 17   A pie chart showing percentages of a publishing company's total annual sales by category of customers

Pareto analysis, charts and diagrams

Pareto analysis is an extremely important tool for prioritizing problems and distinguishing the significant few from the insignificant many. It is based on the work of an Italian economist who discovered a common principle of statistical distribution: that a relatively large number of effects (roughly 80 per cent) arise from a relatively small number of causes (roughly 20 per cent). This principle applies to a great many situations, and is often called the 80/20 Rule. In business terms, for example, 80 per cent of sales often come from 20 per cent of customers, or 8 per cent of problems arise from 2 per cent of causes. Knowing whether, and how, the Pareto rule applies in your operations can allow you to concentrate efforts on the important, high-value factors that will yield the best results. Joseph Juran places great emphasis on Pareto analysis.

Pareto charts present information in tabular form. A chart must show:

- the overall number of an occurrence (for example, an error or sale)
- the relative percentage of that occurrence in the total
- the cumulative number of all occurrences in the total
- the cumulative percentage of occurrences in the total

Using the example of the error chart from Figure 12, Figure 18 illustrates a Pareto chart.

Error	Frequency	Relative %	Cumulative frequency	Cumulative %
Slow service	84	40.8	84	40.8
Teller error	44	21.4	128	62.2
Clerical error	35	17.0	163	79.2
Lost paperwork	21	10.2	184	89.4
Lack of courtesy	12	5.8	196	95.2
Computer error	6	2.9	202	98.1
Other	4	1.9	206	100.0
Total	206	100.0		

Figure 18   Error chart data shown as a Pareto chart

Pareto diagrams are histograms which have been arranged to show the numerical value of the elements in descending order. This allows managers to identify the significant 80 per cent of the elements in question, and focus their attention on these. Figure 19 shows the data from the error chart in the form of a Pareto diagram.

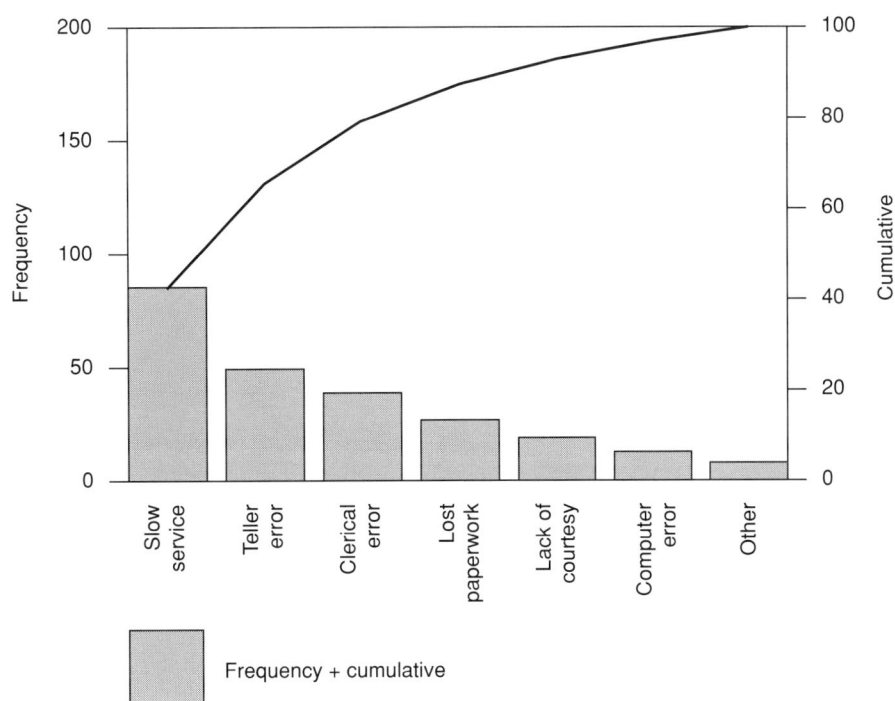

Figure 19   Error chart data shown as a Pareto diagram

Fishbone diagrams

Fishbone diagrams are also called cause-and-effect diagrams or Ishikawa diagrams after their Japanese inventor. They are designed to identify the root causes of problems (rather than merely the symptoms). Unlike histograms, Pareto analysis or scatter diagrams, fishbone diagrams are not primarily designed to present or analyse statistical information. Instead they rely on the simple technique of examining an issue or problem in terms of its constituent parts and repeatedly asking 'why? what caused this?'. They are thus a good tool for analysing complex or chronic problems affected by a number of influences. They provide a useful structure for examining qualitative information, including the human factors affecting a situation.

The fishbone diagram takes its name from the shape of the structure used to identify and record causes. The name of the problem is written at the 'head' of the fish, and the various causes written on the 'ribs' along its spine. The range of causes to be examined should include the 'PEM/PEM' prompts (People-Environment-Methods; Plant-Equipment-Materials); the 4M prompts (Men-Machines-Methods-Material); or whatever combination is appropriate to the particular problem. The quality improvement group brainstorms as many ideas relating to these categories as possible, persisting in asking 'why?' until the underlying cause is identified. If the group's understanding of the problem is very unfocused, a number of separate fishbone diagrams analysing each category will need to be constructed before its underlying causes are identified. Figure 20 illustrates a simple fishbone diagram.

90 word not used

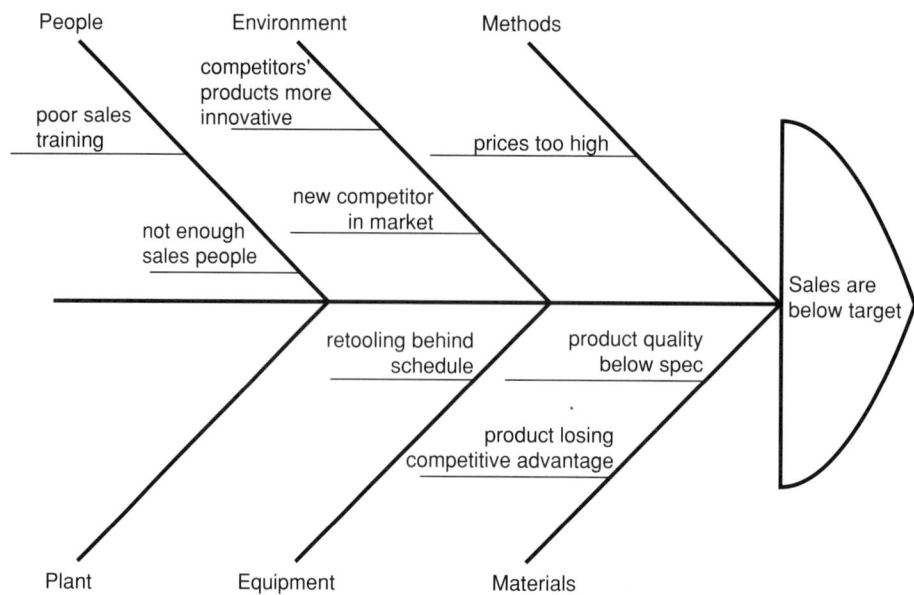

Figure 20   A fishbone diagram starting to analyse a marketing problem

Scatter diagrams

Scatter diagrams are also concerned with cause and effect relationships, but use statistical data to identify them. A scatter diagram focuses on the correlation between two process parameters, an independent parameter (that is, the one that is not affected by the other) and a 'dependent' parameter (the one that varies in some relationship to the independent one).

The dependence or independence of parameters are relative to each situation. If you are investigating the percentage of defects in manufactured parts per shift, you could construct a diagram in which the independent parameter would be the number of parts manufactured during a shift, and the dependent parameter would be the number of defects occurring in these parts. You would be looking for correlations between the number of defects and the number of parts manufactured per shift. The defects will either be a relatively constant percentage of the overall number of parts, or they will increase or decrease in a disproportionate way to the number of parts completed per shift.

Scatter diagrams (see Figure 21) indicate whether a correlation exists, and whether it is strong or weak. It is up to the problem-solving team to interpret and analyse the character and causes of the correlation. If one factor is dependent on another, controlling the independent factor will be a way of controlling the independent one.

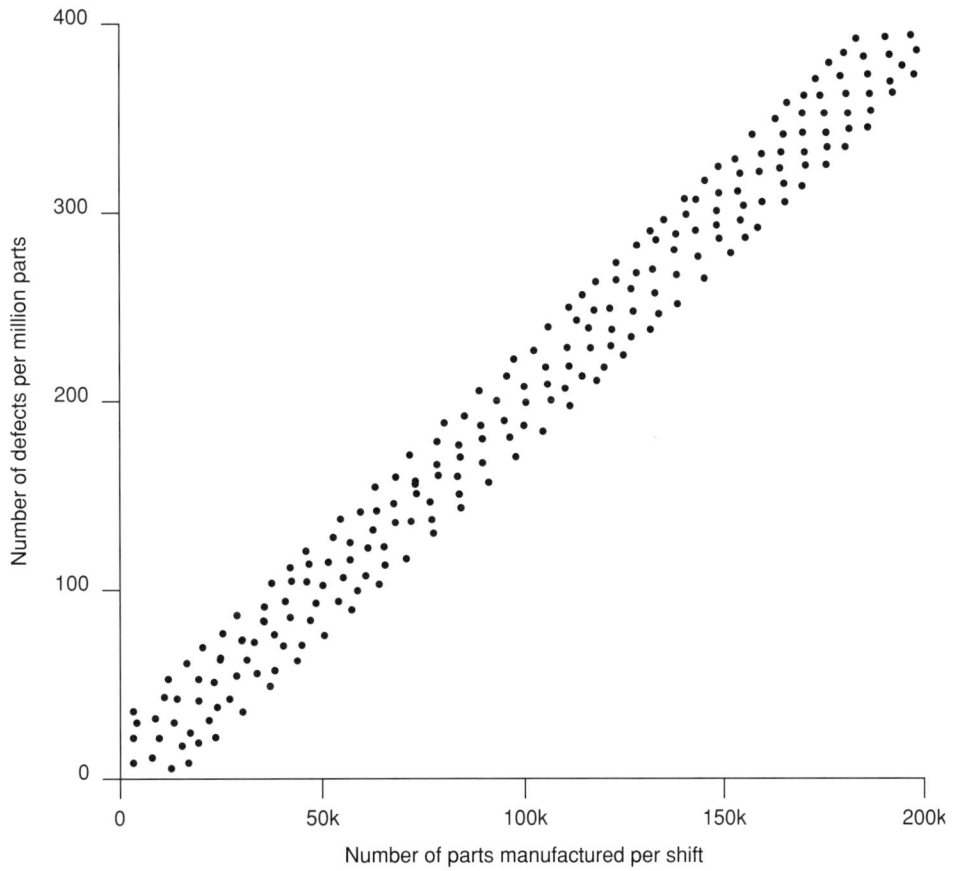

Figure 21   A scatter diagram showing a strong correlation between numbers of parts and numbers of defects

---

Return to the process you identified in Activity 31, or select another process if you prefer. Which of the problem-identification and problem-analysis techniques would you use to improve it? Make a list of the most appropriate techniques, then identify the sequence for using them that you feel would yield the best results.

Solving problems

There are two key principles to solving problems in a Total Quality organization:

- corrective action
- continuous improvement

CORRECTIVE ACTION

Identifying and analysing a problem is a meaningless exercise unless the information generated is used to solve it effectively. There is usually more than one way to solve a particular problem, including short-term and long-term solutions. Meaningful, long-term quality gains can only be achieved if an organization is committed not merely to implementing quick fixes, but to addressing – and eradicating – the root cause of a problem. This is the only approach that will deliver an acceptable return on the investment in a TQM programme. As you saw in Section 1, prevention is always more cost effective than cure.

Often organizations faced with an urgent quality problem do not have the leisure to focus exclusively on the long term. In such cases, if customers need a short-term solution, the organization must provide it. The organization must be careful not to content itself with firefighting, however, but to press on to discover and implement systemic solutions to prevent recurrences.

CONTINUOUS IMPROVEMENT

Total Quality Management is evolutionary, depending on a rolling process of identifying, implementing, consolidating and evaluating quality improvements. In practical terms there are several aspects to continuous improvement:

- continuing to identify incremental improvements to existing procedures and processes (for example, dealing with lower-priority issues, after the higher-priority ones (those delivering the 80 per cent returns) have been dealt with)
- continuing to monitor customer requirements and expectations so that products and processes can be modified in line with them
- using problem-solving techniques to identify innovations and improvements that are not 'problems' (except that they are not yet being used to optimize resources and maximize quality)

- monitoring the changes already introduced as a result of process management, in order to assess whether, and to what extent, they actually do produce measurable improvements

The aim of continuous improvement is to achieve a spiral of increasing quality by embedding the techniques of process management into the operational systems of the organization.

The following activity helps you to consolidate your learning in this section.

ACTIVITY 37

1   Name the main elements of a process diagram.

2   What two aspects of any process activity should be measured? Name three dimensions against which each could be measured.

3   Outline the purpose and main principle behind run charts and process control charts.

4   What are the four phases of a process investigated by statistical process control?

5   Name two techniques which are suitable for analysing qualitative information.

6   Outline the principle behind Pareto analysis, and describe Pareto charts and Pareto diagrams.

7   When would you use scatter diagrams?

8   What is the fishbone diagram designed to identify?

9   When would it be more helpful to use a histogram instead of a pie chart, and vice versa?

FEEDBACK

If you had difficulties with any question in the previous activity, refresh your memory by re-reading the relevant section. Or you might find it useful to discuss the issue with a colleague.

Summary

- The technical skills of Total Quality Management are used to measure and analyse an organization's key processes so that employees can begin to identify solutions to problems and opportunities for improvement. Techniques such as process analysis, flow charting and statistical process control can help the initial measuring and analysis of key processes.
- Techniques that quality improvement groups can use for identifying and analysing problems and opportunities for improvement include:
    - brainstorming
    - flow charting
    - critical examination matrix
    - histograms and pie charts
    - Pareto analysis, charts and diagrams
    - fishbone diagrams
    - scatter diagrams
- The overall approach to using these technical methods involves:
    - using process analysis and measurement to understand key processes
    - identifying high-priority problems (those that will yield the greatest return)
    - analysing them to identify their root causes

- if necessary, using a temporary, ameliorative approach to solve them in the urgent short term
- taking a corrective action approach to eradicate the root causes of problems and prevent their recurrence
- using continuous improvement to keep identifying high-priority problems and ultimately to address lower-priority problems

Note

1 *The Improvement Process*, Harrington (1987), p. 103.

Section 6
Monitoring and evaluating results

Introduction

In this section of the workbook you will consider the issue of monitoring and evaluating the results of your Total Quality Management initiative. It will give you an overview of the key performance indicators you will need to keep track of and assess, including improvements in product quality, in the quality of relationships with important stakeholders, and in poor-quality costs. The section also looks at the question of measuring apparently intangible factors such as employee morale, teamwork and communication.

As you saw in Section 5, measuring and assessing results are meaningless unless the information they produce is used to guide action. This section discusses ways in which performance data on the TQM process can be fed back into the continuous improvement loop. Finally, it offers some guidance on how to maintain the momentum of your quality programme by effectively communicating review results and by keeping a balance between the 'hard', technical and 'soft', human-relations management aspects of Total Quality Management.

WHERE THIS SECTION FITS

As you saw in Section 1, review is one of the key stages of a Total Quality Management programme. In the review stage, actual performance is compared with the goals and objectives set in the planning stage. Information from review activities is a crucial element in the continuous improvement process. It not only reveals the level of progress already attained, but also helps identify further areas for improvement and clarifies whether the goals themselves should be revised or reprioritized.

Key performance indicators

Because the improvement process in a Total Quality organization is ongoing, it is sometimes difficult to decide where process management ends and review activities begin. In fact review activities are more global and are designed to assess the results of the TQM process itself. Review is a rolling procedure. Departmental reviews should be conducted at least quarterly by department heads, and a larger review held annually either by an independent auditor or by the TQM management team acting on behalf of the senior quality council.

Whatever type of enterprise your organization is involved in, your TQM programme will aim to:

- increase quality
- decrease poor-quality costs

Both of these overall performance indicators will need to be assessed in the review process.

QUALITY IMPROVEMENTS

Increased quality can be demonstrated in terms of:

- product or service quality
- quality of relationships with internal and external customers
- quality of relationships with suppliers
- the quality of the working life of your employees

As you saw earlier in the workbook, real quality gains occur when any of these areas show improvement without causing a deterioration in any other area. In practice, the Total Quality objectives for your organization are likely to include goals and targets in each of these areas.

ACTIVITY 38   F4, F5

You can complete the following satisfaction assessment to evaluate the effect of your organization's Total Quality initiative on key stakeholders. If you are still planning your TQM initiative, you can use this checklist to help you identify appropriate goals for your programme to work towards.

		Yes	No
The external customers' point of view			
1	Has the quality of your product/s improved in terms of:		
	■ design?	❏	❏
	■ performance?	❏	❏
	■ reliability?	❏	❏
	■ durability?	❏	❏
	■ ease of use?	❏	❏
	■ after-sales service?	❏	❏
	■ guarantees or warranties?	❏	❏
	■ packaging?	❏	❏
2	Has price decreased, either in real terms or in relation to the rate of inflation, the Retail Price Index, key competitors' products, or some other meaningful yardstick?	❏	❏
3	Has your product's value to the customer increased?	❏	❏
4	Has customer service improved?	❏	❏
The internal customer's point of view			
1	Has the quality of output among departments increased?	❏	❏
2	Have departmental fortresses diminished?	❏	❏
3	Has the quality of relationships (expressed in terms of communication, trust, understanding and co-operation) improved between departments?	❏	❏
Your suppliers' point of view			
1	Do your suppliers feel their relationship with your organization has improved?	❏	❏
2	Are your orders to them established on a more secure basis?	❏	❏
3	Have you helped them develop specifications and processes to meet your requirements?	❏	❏
4	Have you helped them with, or advised them on, training?	❏	❏
Your employees' point of view			
1	Are employees at all levels enjoying their jobs more?	❏	❏
2	Has teamwork improved?	❏	❏
3	Has their self-esteem increased as a result of empowerment and close involvement in improving quality?	❏	❏
4	Have absenteeism and staff attrition at all levels decreased?	❏	❏

POOR-QUALITY COSTS

Poor-quality costs, as you saw in Section 1, can be expressed in terms of:

■ prevention costs
■ appraisal costs
■ failure costs
■ the relationship between these as proportions of the overall poor-quality cost

The management team of your Total Quality programme, advised by the finance department and, perhaps, by your management consultants, will need to devise appropriate ways of measuring and evaluating these costs in your organization. The checklist in Activity 38 will help you evaluate your TQM programme in terms of its impact on poor-quality costs.

ACTIVITY 39

1　Have poor-quality costs gone down overall since the TQM initiative began?

2　What proportion of overall poor-quality costs are represented by:
■ prevention costs?

■ appraisal costs?

■ failure costs?

3　Has there been an improvement in these proportions, i.e. do prevention costs represent an increasing proportion of overall poor-quality costs, with failure costs representing the smallest proportion of the overall total?

Other important financial assessments of the performance of the TQM initiative will include:

■ increases in turnover
■ increases in profits
■ return on investment

This information will be of primary interest to another important group of stakeholders in the organization: the owners or shareholders.

It is important to have realistic expectations about improvements in poor-quality costs. Harrington's rule of thumb is that TQM programmes can cut such costs by roughly one-third over a three-year period. Not allowing enough time for emerging quality gains to reach the bottom line is the equivalent of spoiling the ship for a pennyworth of tar. At the same time, it is essential to monitor results rigorously and consistently, so that unworkable measures are abandoned and the organization does not throw good money after bad. The difficult balance between these two extremes is an area where organizations in the early years of a TQM programme can feel most bewildered, and one where the guidance of reliable management consultants can be very valuable.

The review process should look at the overall performance of the quality initiative, looking for **improvements** in:

- customer satisfaction
- turnover
- profits
- productivity
- use of resources
- decision making
- employee morale
- company image

It should also look for **reductions** in:

- complaints
- warranty claims
- design changes
- delays at internal hand-over points
- scrap, rework and failures
- through-put time
- confusion
- frustration
- wasted time

Measuring the human resource gains

One place where an organization can expect demonstrable quality gains well before the three-year limit is in the 'soft objectives' area of human resource management. Organizational objectives in this area may include improvements in morale, teamwork and communication, as a result of the empowerment measures used in the quality initiative.

At first glance, it may seem difficult to find ways of measuring such apparently intangible elements, but a number of measures can be devised, including:

- employee morale surveys (such as the one in Figure 7, p. 47)
- evaluation of absenteeism
- evaluation of staff attrition records

Attitude surveys and other forms of evaluation should be conducted before, during and after the implementation stage. This will give a good indication of the morale in the organization, and of how it changes as the TQM initiative progresses.

It is unlikely that morale will improve straight away. In fact, it is realistic to expect that it may even decline for a period during the planning and implementation stages. Change programmes are stressful, and, as you saw in Section 3, many people tend to fear and resist change in the workplace. Openness, good communications, empowerment, and effective training in the 'soft skills' should help to minimize negative reactions and to promote gains in teamwork, morale and communication. Managers should monitor the human resource indicators carefully and take prompt remedial action if employee morale appears to be going into free-fall.

Activity 40 provides a framework for assessment and action planning in the area of 'soft objectives'.

ACTIVITY 40   F4, F6

You can use this activity either as a prompt to help you in the planning phase, or as a review tool if your organization's TQM programme has reached the review stage.

Assessment form for empowerment and other human resource objectives

1 Are our efforts in this area working?

2 How do we know this?

3 Are our efforts in this area delivering sufficient gains against objectives?

4 Where are the areas of greatest success?

5 Where are the areas of least success?

6 What can we learn from this?

7 What measures can we take to extend the best results into less successful areas?

8 Would this entail any additional (or different) measurement/evaluation procedures?

Acting on review results

Implementing a Total Quality Management programme is a process itself, one – as you will appreciate by now – with many subprocesses. The data produced by measuring the effectiveness of the TQM process (and subprocesses) must be investigated and analysed in just the same way that information from an error logging chart, for example, is analysed.

Management teams conducting reviews will work backwards from the raw data to trace the causes of the various results revealed by the measurements. Managers can use a number of the analysis techniques discussed in Section 5 (fishbone diagrams, for example) to draw out the lessons from both successes and disappointments. Only in this way can the information be plundered for its potential to reveal possible improvements. As with any other process-management information, no benefit is gained unless the information is fed back into the process to achieve improved performance.

There are two major ways review information can be fed back into quality improvement systems:

- to identify areas where current measures are not working, or are not performing optimally, and therefore should be changed
- to identify areas where measures are successful and might be introduced into other parts of the organization

As you saw in Section 1, one of the factors that distinguishes successful TQM organizations from less successful ones is the ability to capitalize on quality gains by applying new learning throughout the organization. For example, one educational institution discovered that a mentoring system originally developed for clerical workers could be adapted for use by academics and senior administrators. Quality-enhancing know-how can sometimes transfer around an organization in unexpected ways, for example a principle or procedure that works well on an assembly line can be adapted for use in the IT or finance department.

Both obvious and less obvious ways of recycling successful techniques should be explored. Once a Total Quality programme has been running long enough to produce some clear results, both management and operational quality improvement groups can examine the successful approaches used in other parts of the organization, to see if they can be applied in their own areas. Lateral thinking and brainstorming techniques can be used to develop ways to apply current know-how in innovative ways.

Regular exchanges of information among quality improvement groups can aid the cross-fertilization of ideas. A questionnaire such as the one shown in Activity 41 can be used on a regular basis, for example quarterly, to facilitate this process.

ACTIVITY 41

The following questionnaire should be filled in regularly and circulated to other quality improvement groups in the organization.

Quality improvement team questionnaire

1 What is the most valuable improvement your team has implemented recently?

2 What applications do you see for it in other areas?

3 What is the most useful technical skill your team has learned/used recently?

4 What applications do you see for it in other areas?

5 What is the most useful interpersonal or teamworking skill your team has used/learned recently?

6 What applications do you see for it in other areas?

Activity 42 provides an overall framework for examining and learning from the performance results of processes.

ACTIVITY 42   F4

Quality improvement groups can use brainstorming and other problem-analysis techniques to answer the following questions in order to evaluate processes and subprocesses.

Process evaluation checklist

1 On a scale of 1 to 10, how successful is the performance of this process (or subprocess) against objectives?

2 If poor, why?

3 If good, why?

4 If poor, how can we:

   ■ improve the situation?

   ■ prevent problems recurring in this area?

   ■ prevent this problem in other areas of the organization?

5 If good, how can we:
   ■ maintain these quality gains?

   ■ further improve quality gains?

6 If good, how can we introduce the principles or practices from this process into other areas of the organization, by, for example:

   ■ taking improvements further toward the beginning of the process chain (e.g. the design phase)?

   ■ taking improvements into other parts of the organization that use the same or similar processes?

   ■ taking improvements into other functional areas?

   ■ taking improvements into other groups of employees or levels of the management structure?

- taking improvements into our relationships with internal customers, external customers, suppliers or other stakeholders?

7   How should the original objectives set for this process be amended in the light of performance to date?

8   How should the overall priority of the objectives set for this process be amended in the light of performance to date?

Maintaining the momentum

COMMUNICATING RESULTS

It can be difficult, over time, to maintain momentum and enthusiasm for a Total Quality initiative. One important use for review information is to help with this issue. The results of monitoring and evaluation processes, whether from routine quarterly assessments or from annual audits, should be communicated to employees in the way that is both most meaningful to them and best designed to maintain their commitment and pride in the quality programme. This entails the use of different information for different sections of the organization. For example, senior managers and executives are likely to respond most favourably to overall indicators of improved business performance and bottom-line gains. Operational employees will probably tend to relate better to more 'local' information about improvements in their own work areas.

Evaluation results should form an important part of the overall communication strategy for the TQM programme. This is especially important after the programme has been running for some time and interest may be beginning to flag. As you saw in Section 3, both departmental and organization-wide successes should be publicized and celebrated.

Disappointments or downright failures should not be swept under the carpet, but discussed openly with employees in terms of the lessons that can be learned from them and the measures that will be taken to redress them. Managers should take care to ensure that a positive note is struck even when discussing unsatisfactory results, and that these are not allowed to overshadow areas of better performance or damage morale. The message that TQM measures processes, not people, should be reiterated, and no blame or stigma attached to the department in question. A tone of 'We must drive our-selves even harder!' must be avoided, and management should emphasize the steps that are being taken to investigate and correct the cause of the dis-appointing results.

ACTIVITY 43

What ways of communicating review information effectively to various employee groups do you think would work best in your organization? Outline an approach for:

■ front-line employees and workteams
■ middle managers
■ senior managers

RETAINING A BALANCED APPROACH

Effective TQM initiatives maintain momentum by working for quality improvements from both ends of the organizational hierarchy. As John Macdonald points out, programmes driven solely from either the top down or the bottom up are unlikely to continue achieving quality gains over the long haul. Senior-management-led, top-down programmes over-emphasize the long-term, evolutionary gains made by training managers and changing organizational culture. They tend to promote an atmosphere in which every-one is waiting around for the cultural and educational changes to occur at management level, before practical steps are taken to improve quality on the shop floor.

Conversely, TQM programmes that emphasize the bottom-up approach place too much stress on introducing technical measures at opera-tional level, without addressing necessary changes to management attitudes and practices. Without these changes, such as empowerment, the short-term quality gains initiated on the shop floor will wither for lack of management support.

Figures 22, 23 and 24 illustrate Macdonald's recommendation of an integrated approach.

This is another way of saying that the technical 'hard' approach and the interpersonal, 'soft' approach must be balanced and work in tandem, with neither gaining ground at the expense of the other.

Culture- and training-led
Long-term focus
Global aims

Operational level of quality
management is postponed

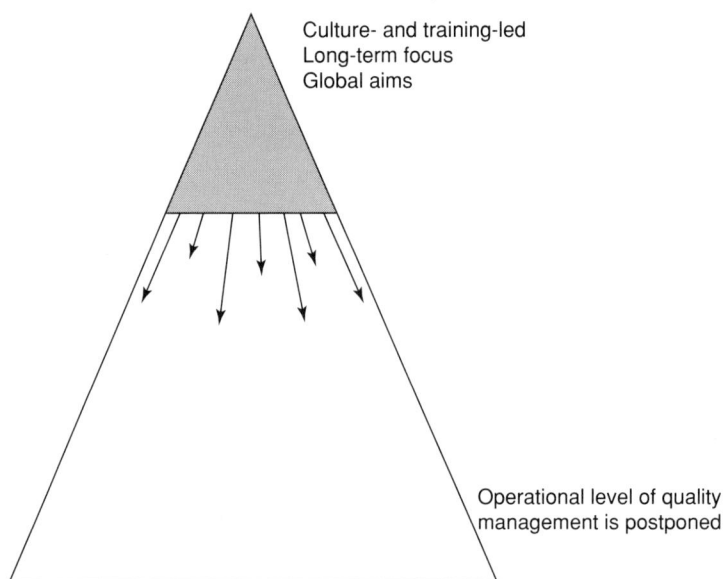

Figure 22   A TQM programme driven by the culture-change approach

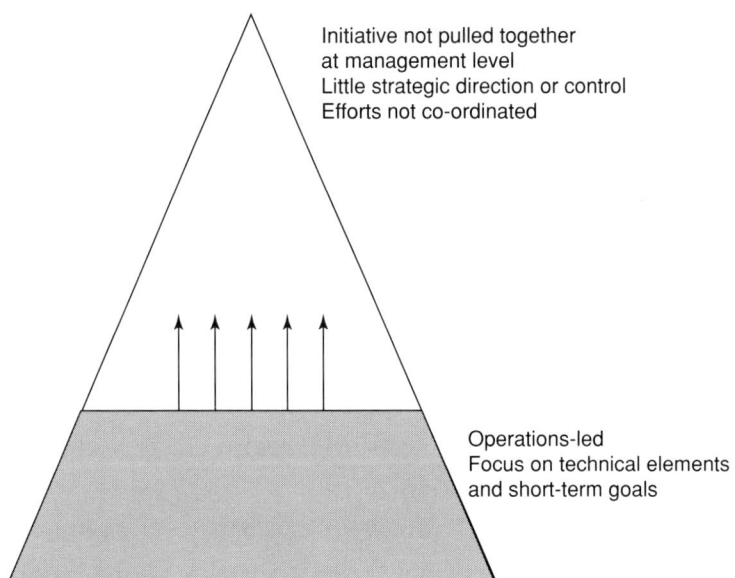

Initiative not pulled together
at management level
Little strategic direction or control
Efforts not co-ordinated

Operations-led
Focus on technical elements
and short-term goals

Figure 23   A TQM programme driven by the technical approach

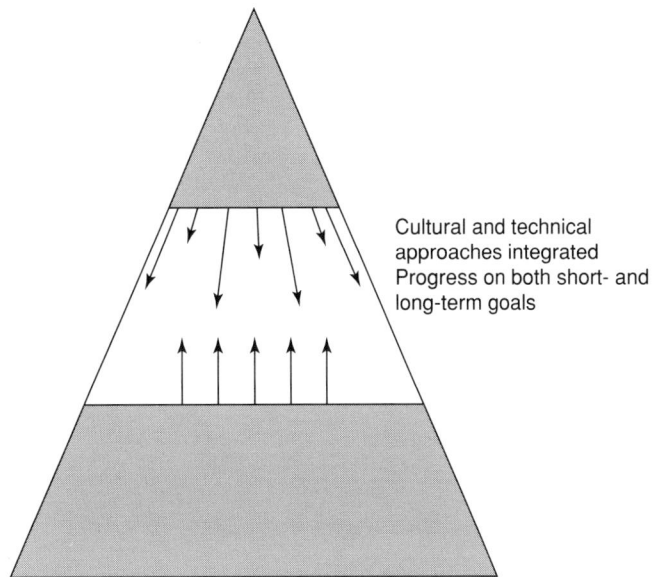

Cultural and technical
approaches integrated
Progress on both short- and
long-term goals

Figure 24   A TQM programme with the technical and cultural approaches well integrated

---

ACTIVITY 43

If your organization is planning a TQM initiative, which of the two aspects of Total Quality Management, the process management side or the human resource management side, will it have to work harder to introduce and maintain?

If your organization is currently engaged in a Total Quality Management programme, which of these aspects (if either) currently appears to be the dominant one?

The following activity helps you to consolidate your learning in this section.

ACTIVITY 45

1   What two general performance indicators should the review stage assess?

2   Name five key groups of stakeholders in an organization's Total Quality programme.

3   What two overall objectives will a Total Quality organization have regarding its poor-quality costs?

4   What is a reasonable expectation of performance in reducing poor-quality costs over time?

5   Name three ways of measuring human resource indicators such as morale, teamwork and communication.

6   Name four potential ways in which successful quality-enhancing know-how might be extended further into an organization.

7   Outline the most effective way to communicate the results of a review of the quality programme to the members of an organization.

8   What is the risk in focusing too exclusively on the cultural, HR aspects of Total Quality Management?

9   What is the risk in focusing too exclusively on the technical, operational aspects of Total Quality Management?

If you had difficulties with any question in the previous activity, refresh your memory by re-reading the relevant section. Or you might find it useful to discuss the issue with a colleague.

Summary

- Review is one of the key phases of a Total Quality Management programme. The review stage allows an organization to assess how well the initiative is progressing against the objectives set in the planning phase. Overall, the review stage evaluates the increases in quality and decreases in poor-quality costs achieved by the initiative.

- Information about performance in these areas must be fed back into the quality improvement cycle, and used to analyse both successes and failures. The insight gained from evaluation can be used to:
    - modify procedures that are not producing satisfactory results
    - amend existing targets, objectives and priorities, or set new ones
    - identify new applications for successful measures, so that the organization's investment in quality gains can be optimized

- The momentum of a Total Quality programme can be maintained by communicating review results to various sectors of the organization in a way best designed to maintain commitment and boost morale. Another important factor in maintaining impetus is to keep the two major aspects of Total Quality Management, the technical, operational side and the cultural, human relations management side, in dynamic balance

Summary

On completion of this workbook you should have gained knowledge and techniques in the following:

- TQM is a holistic management approach
- TQM is based around a five-stage process
- selecting approaches to TQM
- choosing between 'big bang' and incremental approaches
- the importance of people management skills, and changing culture
- technical skills for measuring effectiveness of processes, and problem solving
- techniques for monitoring and evaluating performance

Appendix The quality gurus

Since its early beginnings in the 1950s, quality improvement or total quality management has given rise to various people whose beliefs, ideologies and theories have been proven to be successful in turning below-average companies into successful businesses, mediocre companies into excellent companies, and good companies into the world's best. These people have been termed 'gurus' in recognition of their expertise.

Each of the 'gurus' has his own theory of how a total culture or programme may be introduced and sustained. Whilst there are obvious similarities in their approaches there are also differences which make each of the gurus distinctive.

It is important to note that the theories which helped to change post-war Japan did not come from Japan itself, but from the minds of Americans, in particular Dr W. Edwards Deming and Dr Joseph Moses Juran.

Today, there are many quality and total quality consultants but only a handful of recognized gurus. This handful includes Deming, Juran, Crosby, Feigenbaum, Ishikawa and Taguchi and they are probably the most renowned and revered of all Quality experts.

This appendix will look briefly at some of these gurus.

Dr W. Edwards Deming

Deming was a hero in Japan for some thirty years before he was given recognition in his homeland – the USA. This happened in June 1980 when he broadcast on NBC on the now famous subject 'if the Japanese can … why can't we?'

Deming's theory centres around the belief that whilst quality is everyone's job, management must lead the effort, independent of the size of the organization or sector of the market. He is also an enthusiastic campaigner for training and believes that there can be no substitute for knowledge. This is clearly reflected in his classic 14 points for industrial revival and transformation.

DEMING'S 14 POINTS

1 Create constancy of purpose
2 Adopt a new philosophy
3 Cease dependence on inspection
4 Stop awarding business on price
5 Improve constantly and forever the system of production and service
6 Institute training on the job
7 Institute leadership
8 Drive out fear
9 Break down inter-departmental barriers
10 Eliminate slogans, exhortations and numerical targets
11 Eliminate quotas or work standards and management by objectives or numerical goods
12 Allow pride of workmanship
13 Institute a vigorous education and self-improvement programme
14 Put everyone in the company to work to achieve the transformation

The 14 points are undoubtedly fine aims or goals. However, it is widely regarded that Deming provides no tools to achieve these goals. They in fact become more of a philosophy than a management practice.

Deming also talks about 'deadly diseases' and 'obstacles' which prevent organizations from performing at the highest levels. These include:

■ Violation of the 14 points
■ Emphasis on short-term profits
■ Mobility of management
■ Performance evaluation

and other parameters such as:

■ Motivation
■ Education
■ Reliance on standards
■ Use of technology

No discussion of Deming, no matter how brief, would be complete without mention of the Deming Cycle. This cycle, also known as the PDCA (plan, do, check, act) cycle, may be used as a helpful procedure for making improvements.

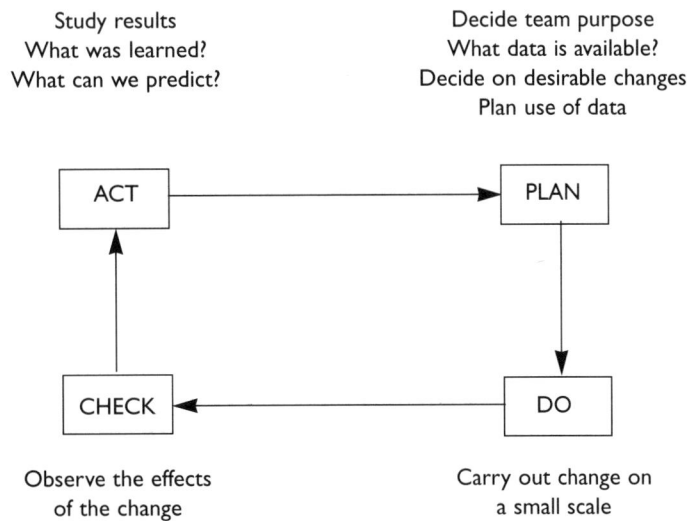

Study results   Decide team purpose
What was learned?   What data is available?
What can we predict?   Decide on desirable changes
                                       Plan use of data

```
  ACT  ──────────────▶  PLAN
   ▲                      │
   │                      │
   │                      ▼
 CHECK ◀───────────────  DO
```

Observe the effects   Carry out change on
of the change   a small scale

Figure A1

Joseph Moses Juran

Juran was a pioneer of quality education in Japan and like Deming remained relatively unknown in the USA until the 1980s. His research has shown that over 80 per cent of quality defects are management controllable and, there-fore, it is management that needs to change.

Juran bases this path to success on the quality trilogy of **quality planning, quality control** and **quality improvement.**

Proper quality planning results in a process which is capable of meeting quality goals under operating conditions.

THE PLANNING ROAD MAP

1　Identify customers
2　Determine the needs of the customers
3　Translate those needs into the organization's language
4　Develop a product to meet those needs
5　Optimize the product features to meet organizational needs as well as customer needs
6　Develop a process capable of producing the product
7　Optimize the process
8　Prove the process under operating conditions
9　Transfer the process to operations

Juran sees quality control resulting in the conduct of operations in accordance with the quality plan. Quality improvement ensures that the conduct of operations achieves a quality level in excess of the planned performance.

All three programmes are dependent on people with specialist skills and knowledge. In the past this specialist knowledge has been limited to managers and engineers in the quality department. Juran insists on a break with tradition and the devising of a quality programme to involve every employee.

This training programme heavily emphasizes the importance of the customer, whether internal or external, or indeed the end user. He illustrates this idea through his 'quality spiral'.

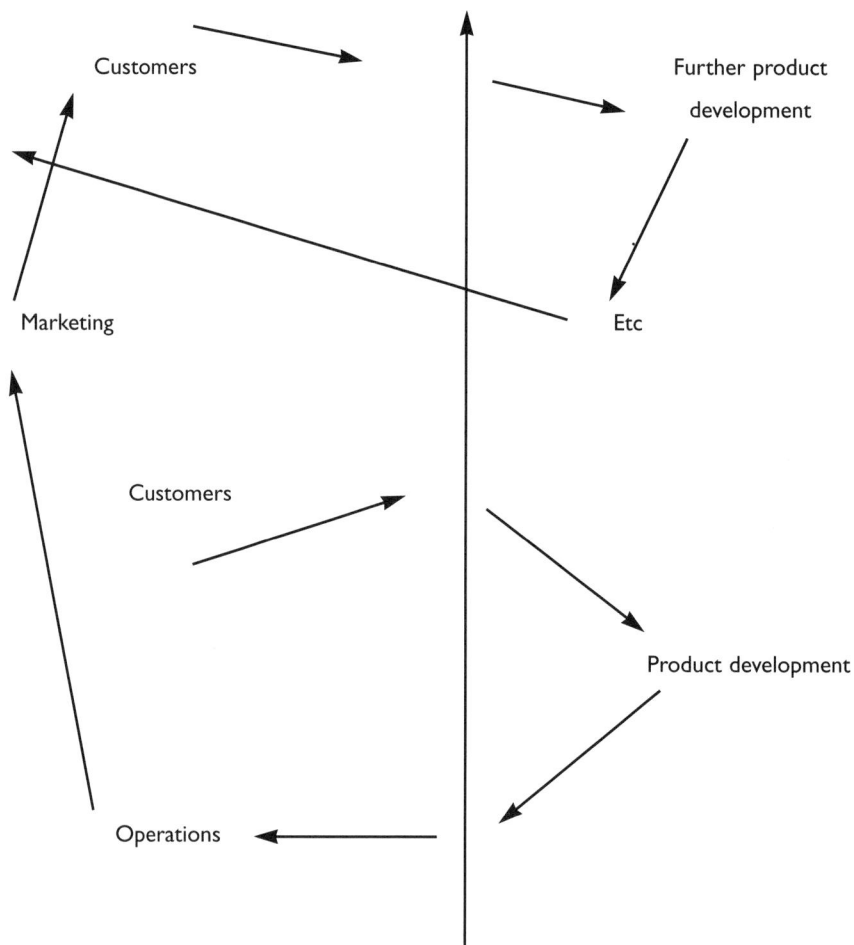

Figure A2

The parameters affecting the external customer must be based on meeting competition in the marketplace, while those affecting the internal customer are based on getting rid of internal waste. The quality programme should incorporate statistical process control techniques within its training remit.

It is apparent that a high percentage of quality improvement programmes fail to achieve their full potential or simply fail altogether. Tom Peters says that 98 per cent of all such programmes fail. Juran suggests that this is due to:

- No detailed identification tasks
- No hierarchy of responsibility
- No structured process of 'how' to tackle the tasks
- No suitable management performance review

However, Juran does present his formula for results as follows:

- Establish specific goals
- Establish plans to reach these goals
- Assign clear responsibility for meeting goals
- Base rewards on results achieved

There are no short cuts to quality, and Juran insists that the majority of problems are the fault of poor management rather than poor workmanship.

Philip B. Crosby

Crosby is best known for developing the programme known as 'zero defects' and his belief that 'quality is free'. He suggests that the things which cost an organization money are all the things that prevent jobs being done right the first time. So when the proper corrective action is taken, these cost areas may be removed.

Crosby proposes 5 absolutes of quality management

1 Quality should be developed as conforming to requirements, not as 'goodness' or 'elegance'
2 The system for causing quality is prevention not detection
3 The performance standard must be zero defects
4 The measurement of quality is the price of not conforming
5 There is no such thing as a quality problem

These absolutes are the basis of his 14-step **quality improvement process** which tackles the following areas:

1 Management commitment
2 Quality improvement teams
3 Quality measurement
4 Cost of quality
5 Quality awareness

6 Corrective action
7 Ad hoc committee for the zero defects programme
8 Supervisor/employee training
9 Zero defects day
10 Goal setting
11 Error cause removal
12 Recognition
13 Quality councils
14 Do it all over again

Crosby suggests that his zero defects policy is based on the presumption that mistakes are caused in two ways:

1 Lack of knowledge
2 Lack of attention

The first problem is relatively easily tackled by provision of an adequate on-going training programme. However, Crosby sees the second problem as being caused by an attitude problem. This attitude can be changed only by the individual and Crosby recognizes that if the individual makes the changes then he/she is more likely to be committed to that change.

Critics of Crosby imply that his 14-step approach lacks practicality and also that his absolutes ignore the concept of continuous improvement. Crosby, however, argues that continuous improvement is a requirement that must be established by management and that the performance standard would involve all employees constantly improving their work processes.

This requirement suggests that total quality management (TQM) has implications for all aspects of organizational culture (this will be discussed in a later section in more detail).

The implementation of TQM must be designed to fit the organizational culture.

Kaoru Ishikawa

As with other Japanese quality gurus, Ishikawa has paid specific attention to making statistical techniques available to industry. Essentially, his work has emphasized good data collection techniques and also suitable presentation methods. His use of Pareto charts and the development of the Ishikawa or fishbone (cause and effect) diagram as an analytic tool brought him to the fore of Japan's quality drive in the 1950s and 1960s.

Ishikawa is associated with **company-wide quality control** whereby quality is characterized by company-wide participation from top management through everyone in the organization tree. Importantly, everyone in the company should study statistical methods.

Ishikawa stresses that the word 'quality' does not apply simply to the product but to every aspect of the business, e.g. design, engineering, research, finance, sales, marketing, the company itself and the human beings. Bearing these ideas in mind the Ishikawa approach results in:

1 Reduced defects
2 Improved reliability
3 Reduced costs
4 Increased production
5 Reduction of wasteful work
6 Improved techniques
7 Reduced inspection and testing costs
8 Rationalized contracts between the vendor and vendee
9 Enlarged sales market
10 Better interdepartmental relationships
11 Reduction of false data and reports
12 More democratic discussions
13 Smoother meetings
14 Better repairs and installation of equipment
15 Better human relations

QUALITY CIRCLES

One aspect of Ishikawa's company-wide quality control is the practice of quality circles. These circles constitute a voluntary group of around 6–8 people from the same work area. The group meets regularly and is led by a supervisor or a team member. The aims of the quality circle are as follows:

- To make improvements and help develop the organization
- To respect human relations and create a good team atmosphere
- To use the normally untapped human potential to the full

Each person on the team, as already suggested, is introduced to and trained in statistical techniques like those listed below:

- Pareto charts
- Cause and effect diagrams
- Stratification
- Check sheets
- Histograms
- Scatter diagrams
- Control charts

Summary

In summary, all of the quality gurus are aiming for the same ideal, i.e. 'perfection'. It is their path to perfection which differs.

While perfection is the aim, they all realize that it is never attainable. What is important is that each person within the organization strives towards making continuous improvements.

All regard management commitment as a fundamental prerequisite to starting a quality improvement programme. Once, and only when this commitment has been gained, should training of the workforce take place.

Differences do appear in the style, content and extent of training from guru to guru. However, all agree that it should involve every employee of the organization and that the training must form part of a life-long programme.

Recommended reading

Bell, Desmond, McBride, Philip and Wilson, George (1994) *Managing Quality*, Institute of Management Foundation/Butterworth-Heinemann

Blair, George and Meadows, Sandy (1996) *Winning at Change*, Institute of Management Foundation/Pitman Publishing

Bower, J. L. (1972) *Managing the Resource Allocation Process*, RD Irwin

British Standards Association (1981) *BS 6143, Guide to the Determination and Use of Quality Costs*, BSI

The Competent Manager series (1994) *Quality, Institute of Management*

Crosby, Philip (1972) *Quality is Free*, McGraw-Hill

Crosby, Philip (1989) *Let's Talk Quality*, McGraw-Hill

Deming, W. E. (1986) *Out of the Crisis*, Massachusetts Institute of Technology

Department of Trade and Industry (1990) *The Quality Gurus*, HMSO

Gitlow, H. and Oppenheim, A. (1989) *Tools and Methods for the Improvement of Quality*, Irwin Press

Hagan, J. T. (1986) *Principles of Quality Costs*, American Society for Quality Control

Harrington, H. James (1987) *The Improvement Process: How America's Leading Companies Improve Quality*, McGraw-Hill

Harrington, H. J., (1991) *Business Process Improvement* McGraw-Hill

'The Race to Quality Improvement', suppl., (1989) *Fortune*

Institute of Management Foundation, *Mapping an Effective Change Programme*, Management checklist 038

Institute of Management Foundation, *Implementing an Effective Change Programme*, Management checklist 040

Ishikawa, Kaoru (1982) *Guide to Quality Control*, Asia Productivity Organization

Juran, Joseph (1988) *Quality Control Handbook*, McGraw-Hill

Macdonald, John (1993) *Understanding Total Quality Management in a Week*, Headway/Institute of Management

Margulies, N. (1973) *Organisational Change, Techniques and Application*, Scott-Foresman

Plunkett, J. J. and Dale, B. G. (1985) *Quality Costs*, Department of Trade and Industry

Sadler, Philip (1995) *Managing Change*, Kogan Page

Useful address

The British Quality Foundation
Vigilant House
120 Wilton Road
London SW1V 1JZ

About the Institute of Management

The mission of the Institute of Management (IM) is to promote the development, exercise and recognition of professional management.

The IM is the leading professional organization for managers. Its efforts and resources are devoted to ensuring the continuing development and success of its members.

At the forefront of management standards, the IM provides a range of services for its members. These include flexible training programmes and a unique range of support services such as career counselling, enquiry and research facilities and preferential prices on IM publications and other IM products.

Further details about the Institute of Management may be obtained from:

Institute of Management
Management House
Cottingham Road
Corby
Northants
NN17 1TT

Telephone 01536 204222

We need your views

We really need your views in order to make the Institue of Management Open Learning Programme an even better learning tool for you. Please take time out to complete and return this questionnaire to Tessa Gingell, Pergamon Open Learning, Linacre House, Jordan Hill, Oxford OX2 8DP.

Name:..

Address:...

....

Title of workbook:...

If applicable, please state which qualification you are studying for. If not, please describe what study you are undertaking, and with which organization or college:

....

Please grade the following out of 10 (10 being extremely good, 0 being extremely poor):

Content: .... Suitability for ability level: ....

Readability: .... Qualification coverage: ....

What did you particularly like about this workbook?

....

Are there any features you disliked about this workbook? Please identify them.

....

Are there any errors we have missed?
If so, please state page number: ....

How are you using the material? For example, as an open learning course, as a reference resource, as a training resource, etc.

....

How did you hear about the Institue of Management Open Learning Programme?:

Word of mouth: Through my tutor/trainer: Mailshot:

Other (please give details):..

Many thanks for your help in returning this form.

Institute of Management Open Learning Programme

This programme comprises seventeen workbooks, each on a core management topic with the latest management thinking, as well as a *User Guide* and a *Mentor Guide*.

Designed for self study through open learning, the workbooks cover all management experience from team building to budgeting, from the skills of self management to manage strategically for organizational success.

TITLE	ISBN	Price
The Influential Manager	0 7506 3662 9	£22.50
Managing Yourself	0 7506 3661 0	£22.50
Getting the Right People to Do the Right Job	0 7506 3660 2	£22.50
Understanding Business Process Management	0 7506 3659 9	£22.50
Customer Focus	0 7506 3663 7	£22.50
Getting TQM to Work	0 7506 3664 5	£22.50
Leading from the Front	0 7506 3665 3	£22.50
Improving Your Organization's Success	0 7506 3666 1	£22.50
Project Management	0 7506 3667 X	£22.50
Budgeting and Financial Control	0 7506 3668 8	£22.50
Effective Financial and Resource Management	0 7506 3669 6	£22.50
Developing Yourself and Your Staff	0 7506 3670 X	£22.50
Building a High Performance Team	0 7506 3671 8	£22.50
The New Model Leader	0 7506 3672 6	£22.50
Making Rational Decisions	0 7506 3673 4	£22.50
Communication	0 7506 3674 2	£22.50
Successful Information Management	0 7506 3675 0	£22.50
User Guide	0 7506 3676 9	£22.50
Mentor Guide	0 7506 3677 7	£22.50
Full set of workbooks plus *Mentor Guide* and *User Guide*	0 7506 3359 X	£370.00

To order: *(Please quote ISBNs when ordering)*

- College Orders: 01865 314333
- Account holders: 01865 314301
- Individual Purchases: 01865 314627

(Please have credit card details ready)

For further information or to request a full series brochure, please contact:

Tessa Gingell on 01865 314477